No Youth... No Church

(Exploring the Decline and Impact of Young People Not Attending Church After High School and College)

DOROTHY L. ODEN

A thesis project submitted
in fulfillment of the requirements
for PhD degree in theology
Parkersburg Bible College
2021

ISBN 979-8-89130-100-9 (paperback)
ISBN 979-8-89130-101-6 (digital)

Christian Faith Publishing
832 Park Avenue
Meadville, PA 16335
www.christianfaithpublishing.com

Printed in the United States of America

Abstract

Exploring the Decline and Impact of Young People Not
Attending Church After High School and College

Dorothy L. Oden

There is a startling decline in the number of teenagers and
young adults attending most Christian churches, especially the
Pentecostal Apostolic churches in America after completion of high
school, entrance into and graduation from college. The purpose of
this research study is to discover the reasons why teenagers and young
people are leaving the church, and what effects there will be on the
church with so many young people turning away from Christianity.
The collection of information will be ascertained through a survey
questionnaire and interviews with young people and pastors. This
study will seek strategies, recommendations, and suggestions that
possibly could be implemented to retain, reclaim, and prevent the
youth from leaving the church in the future.

Parkersburg Bible College

THESIS PROJECT APPROVAL SHEET

GRADE

MENTOR

READER

Acknowledgments

I thank my Lord and Savior Jesus Christ for the opportunity to scholastically fulfill my academic educational goal of receiving a PhD in theology. I would like to thank Dr. Joe Nelson, Sister Kim Fortney, and the staff at Parkersburg Bible College for their support and instructions in completing my studies.

I appreciate and want to say thank-you to the pastors, church leaders, youth leaders, teenagers, and young adults who participated in this research study. Thank you for sharing your life experiences, concerns, and ideals. Your feedback to my questions and questionnaire was invaluable.

As a lifelong learner, I am totally and forever indebted to my husband, Bishop Gerald Oden, my adult daughters Dawn, Denien, and Denita; their husbands, Devin and Arthur; and my three grandchildren Aubrey, Devin Jr., and Amiya for their love, encouragement, and prayers. They have untiringly supported me through my entire educational journey. Thanks for believing in me. I am eternally grateful to you all and to my Lord and savior Jesus Christ.

Contents

Chapter 1

Introduction

Within the Christian churches in America, there is a steady decline every year in the number of young people attending the worship services on Sundays. During the weekdays, the seats and pews are scantily occupied with young people for weekly Bible study. Krejcir's reported statistics in 2007 indicated that nearly 50% of Americans do not have a church home (Krejcir 2007). The absence of teenagers and young people in the church is a phenomenon that is seriously impacting the small, store-front churches more than the large and megachurches.

Unfortunately, this trending phenomenon has exhibited itself to the point that some pastors have had to close the doors of their churches, and they have taken down the church signs over the doorways. Perhaps unknowingly, the resistance or delay on the part of bishops, pastors, elders, and deacons to incorporate young people into the activities of their church has retarded the growth of small, local churches. Preparation, participation, engagement, and training of young people in leadership roles is essential for this present-day generation of believers to continue the future growth and existence of the Pentecostal Apostolic churches.

According to the United States Census Bureau Records, there are nearly four thousand churches every year closing their doors and approximately one thousand new churches springing up (Krejcir 2007). Understanding the causes and effects related to young people leaving the church and closure of small churches is at the root of this exploration. The lack of young people's attendance in the church is impacting the sustainability of many protestant churches across America. An unpleasant sight occurring in established churches is the inevitable sicknesses and deaths of older members. As the older members are disappearing, they are not quickly being replaced by younger new members. Regrettably, this is serious; the church will cease to be an active entity without young people to carry it into the future.

This study explored perceived and actual answers to questions that many people have thought about for years but have not researched. Such questions as the following: (1) What are the reasons that young people are not joining and staying in the churches? (2) Why are teenagers and young adults leaving the churches after they have graduated from high school, started college, or when they have obtained their college degrees? To answer these and other questions, the researcher sought information from survey questionnaire generated on Survey Monkey, authors of books, magazines, and blogs who have previously researched this subject matter regarding the decline of young people attending Christian churches. The methodology utilized incorporated the participation of pastors, youth leaders, youth, and ex-youth members from small Pentecostal Apostolic churches along the northeastern corridor.

The future survival and preservation of the church especially the Pentecostal Apostolic churches currently look bleak according to trends and statistics. We are reminded that there has been a steady decline in the number of young people attending the church. In The *Washington Post* article by Emba (2019), "Millennials are more highly educated and spend more time working than their older counterparts, they have stepped back dramatically from religious activities." Not only are young people leaving Christianity, but they are not coming back according to Emba's survey from 2019. Reportedly, young people are "turning to convenient, low-commitment substitutes for faith and fellowship like astrology, the easy 'spiritualism' of yoga and self-care, posting away on Twitter and playing more games" (electronic games). Attending church, learning about Christ, serving him as Lord and Savior is considered irrelevant to this generation of young people. Some of those raised in the church as well as some young people who never attended church regularly are inventing their own methods of spirituality. One day, when they find out that their way of spirituality or connecting with the universe is not satisfying their spiritual need, hopefully they will come to the church for pastoral care. In the meantime, spiritual-minded leaders in the churches need to create plans of action to evangelize those in their communities, in the prisons, and at homeless shelters to keep the church alive.

Churches nowadays are being challenged intellectually by young people with man-made bizarre philosophies and questions relative to their lifestyle and choices, social ills and conflicts, and political corruption. They claim to look to the church for answers to their questions. Some commented that if they cannot ask their questions in the church, they will leave the church and get answers from other sources. This generations of millennials and generation X are temperamental and bold. They are expecting answers and reasons for everything they ask. So the church must be prepared and educated with up-to-date information to effectually reach and appropriately answer their questions without excuses or hesitation solely because if they cannot find answers at the church, they will seek answers from the world.

Despite adults in the church being viewed as teachers and overseers, they can learn some things from young people in their congregation. Young people can teach and assist adults. They are quite knowledgeable, and they are fast learners. They can search the internet quickly for information on countless subjects online to bring the local churches into the twenty-first century. This is an era of computerization and technology. Most adults are not tech savvy as young people. Intergenerational collaboration can promote interest and participation from the youth and ensure the progression of the church into the future. Young people attract young people. Therefore, it is critical over the next twenty years for new young people to come into and join the Pentecostal Apostolic churches. If the young people are not accepted and treated with respect and invited to engage in a timely manner with adults, in service and activities going on in the churches, many churches will see more empty pews in their congregations; young people are leaving the church without saying a word to anyone.

Background of the Problem

The purpose of this research study was to explore the phenomenon behind the causes of teenagers and young adults leaving the church. To ascertain the perceived impact and effects their absence would have on the growth and sustainability of the church in future years.

Going back about twenty to thirty years ago, the houses of the Lord were full of ambitious, active, energetic children, teenagers, and young adults. No one, back then, considered that there would come a period time when young people would be leaving the church. The thought of young people walking away from the church and rejection of Christ was inconceivable. Any mention of someone backsliding was considered damnable. The fear of God and hell fire was drilled into the very fabric of the church. After all, the population of the church was made up of families, multigenerations of mothers, fathers, grandparents, aunts, uncles, nieces, nephews, and cousins who wanted salvation for themselves and their families and friends.

Back in the day, parents did not send their children alone to church, but they brought them to church. Parents taught their children the Word of God at home. The Lord's prayer was said at schools and some of the classroom teachers reiterated and emphasized the scriptures to their students. Reading and telling Bible stories around the dinner table and at bedtime were common scenes. But times have changes, and families are not sitting down together at home or coming to church together like they used to. The Word of God is not being read often. Some families have said that church is not relevant in their lives, and they have given their children the option of following religiosity or not.

As difficult as it is to acknowledge, our experience with generations of parents, grandparents, and elderly relatives at the church is gradually disappearing. Young people are not trained or prepared to maintain the work of the Lord in many small churches. From personal observation and conversations with pastors and church leaders, there has been a massive exit of teenagers and young adults leaving the church especially after they graduate from high school, enter college, and after they complete college. Quite a few of them are leaving the church, and they are not coming back. This is a devastating blow and a major attack on Christianity globally. Therefore, in order for Christian churches to survive here in America, young people are crucially needed back into the churches for evangelism, for growth, and for sustainability. Without young people attending and participating in the churches, some churches will not grow or exist in ten, fifteen, or twenty years.

Literature Review

This research study aimed to explore the phenomenon surrounding the extraordinary departure of teenagers and young people who have walked away and are walking away from the Christian faith and identify the reasons for the decline and the potential impact on Christian churches in America, especially the Pentecostal Apostolic churches. We will take a look at what Christianity may experience in twenty to forty years from now if teenagers and young adults continue to leave the churches.

This literature review will present prior research materials from experts in the field of religion—those who have collected and analyzed research data. This researcher will present findings from experienced clerics, current articles, internet resources, and books about why so many teenagers and young adults are leaving or have left the Christian churches and why some have vowed not to come back. This study will also review thoughts, recommendations, and suggestions of authors who have previously written on the subject and have worked with young people in different settings. Some of them have completed research on how to keep the youth from leaving the church and how the church can strategically work on bringing them back into the churches.

Pew Research Center

According to an article by the Pew Research Center (2015), "The Future of World Religions: Population Growth Projections, 2010-2050," Christianity is the most far-reaching religion on the planet today. But over the next forty years, it has been predicted that Islam may have as many followers as Christianity, or it could exceed Christianity. The researchers observed and cited eight religious groups around the world; they are labeled as Christianity, Muslims, Hindus, Buddhists, Folk Religions, Other Religions, and Jews. This list included the unaffiliated population, those who do not consider themselves to be religious. The Pew Research Center documented that they spent six years studying the differences among the global religious and nonreligious population in categories of their locations, ages, birth, and death rates. Information gathered was consistent with surveys, censuses, and population registers. World population growth expansion in this article is anticipated to range from 6.2 billion to 9.3 billion from the years of 2010 to 2050 with Christians outnumbering adherents to other organized and folk religions.

Findings reported by these researchers indicate that in 2010, Islam had the youngest group of members actively engaged in their religion compared to other religions. They ranged under the ages of fifteen to fifty-nine. This group is expected to continue to grow because their women are giving birth to more children than the other major religious groups. According to the Pew Research Center (2015), Muslims are having 3.1 children per woman; Christians, 2.7 children per woman; Hindu, 2.4 children per woman; Jewish community, 2.3 children per woman; and the other religions, 1.8 to 1.6 children per woman, these demographics in 2010 covered regions in Africa, Australia, China, Europe, India, Japan, Middle East, and the United States.

This article stated that in some countries, when children grew up, they left the religion that they were brought up in, and it was considered normal behavior for them. While in other parts of the world, it is illegal for adults to abandon or change the religion that they grew up in. It was observed in the United States that some who were not raised as Christians became Christians as well as some who were raised Christians left the faith when they became adults. The religious indecisive action of young people on being in the church or out of the church is projected to continue into future generations. And without firm commitment to Christianity, the decline is inevitable. In the article, seventy countries were surveyed, and it was revealed that many admitted that they left the faith that they were raised up in.

A gap in the article was that it lacked information regarding the Pentecostal Apostolic churches globally and here in the United States. The study was conducted based on a worldwide audience. It covered extensively a vast number of religious populations that worshipped Christ and other deities. It did not provide a cause and effect for youth leaving Christianity. Though Islam is noted to be a rapidly growing population almost equal to Christianity, no documentation was provided why young people are attracted to this religion. My research will continue to forge forward to ascertain why the youth are leaving Christianity and what impact the absence of young people will have on the growth and existence of the church in twenty to forty years.

You Lost Me

David Kinnaman, the president of the Barna Group and the author of this book, *You Lost Me. Why Young Christians Are Leaving Church...And Rethinking Faith*, provides revealing information on the ways young adults view and understand the function of the church in which they are living in. The book gives rise to "concerns, hopes, delusions, frustrations, and disappointments" that young Christians and ex-Christians expressed (Kinnaman 2011). Below are articles written by the Barna Group that showed statistics from participants who answered survey questions over the telephone or online found in this book.

An article written in 2011 by the researchers at the Barna Group delineates "Six Reasons Young Christians Leave Church." The research was conducted over a five-year period with interviews from teenagers, young adults, parents, youth pastors, and senior pastors. They targeted young people who went to church on regular basis and then left the church after they turned fifteen years old. The study recorded that 59% or nearly three out of five of the young Christians strayed away from the church either permanently or temporarily for many different reasons once they grew up (Barna Group, "Six Reasons Young Christians Leave Church," September 27, 2011).

Here are six reasons of young Christians leaving the church outlined in the article:

"Reason #1—Churches seem overprotective." One quarter of the teenagers and young adults surveyed expressed that the church is out of touch with the problems going on in the world. They said activities not based inside of a church was thought of as being of the devil. They were restrictions on going to the movies, listening to music, and playing video games; the church was too overprotective of them. They did not get a chance to do activities outside of the church because the church was afraid that something might happen to them.

This generation of youth are exposed to fast, attractive, imaginative, offensive, and ungodly activities in the world that seems to pull them in. The biggest culprit today is social media platforms and applications. They reveal what people are doing and thinking in many cultures around the world, and often, these activities are unfiltered and uncensored. Without the youth knowing it, these things are impacting their thought processes and frame of mind. The internet connections, whether appropriate or inappropriate, appear to be a great influence on the thought processes of young people connected to the church, and it entices them to desire the pleasures of worldliness.

"Reason #2—Teens' and twentysomethings experience of Christianity is shallow." These respondents who left the church verbalized that the church was not important to them. The teaching of the Bible was not sufficient. To them, it was abstract. They did not experience a spiritual connection or develop a relationship with God while attending the church.

"Reason #3—Churches come across as antagonistic to science." A lot of young people in the church are struggling between believing in the doctrine of creation and the scientific argument of evolution. Many of them believe that the church is ignorant of the role that science plays in our everyday lives. They said that they are having difficulty pursuing and securing employment or starting a career path dealing with science because they do not believe God is in science.

"Reason #4—Young Christians' church experiences related to sexuality are often simplistic, judgmental." Young Christians are tempted to commit fornication and partake in promiscuous behavior due to easy access to pornography on the internet; 17% confessed to engagement in immorality and felt like the church judged them for their indiscretion. They are struggling to live holy lives. Because they are sexually active in church, the trend is that young adults are waiting until late in life to marry.

"Reason #5 -They wrestle with the exclusive nature of Christianity." This group of young Christians, 22% of them, reported that the "church is like a country club, only for insiders." According to those interviewed, the church is not open to accepting or experiencing new ideas and ways of doing things from other cultures or people outside the church as they are. They said that they are not afraid to study or participate in non-Christian ideations, and they were up for the challenge. They also stated that the "churches are afraid of the beliefs of other faiths."

"Reason #6—The church feels unfriendly to those who doubt." Some 36% of the young Christians exclaimed that they were uncomfortable asking questions relating to issues in their personal life and their doubts concerning faith in the church. According to this article, some 18% of the young people affiliated with the church stated that the churches did not provide emotional support or assist in their time of depression (Barna 2011).

This article was informative as it proposed some reasons why America's young people, ages eighteen to twenty-nine, were leaving the church or had left the church. From the comments of the respondents, it appears that they laid blame at the feet of the leaders of the churches for their departures. They apparently felt that the church did not recognize the teenagers and young adults who showed no interest in church or who had disconnected themselves from the faith early on. Statistics has shown that there are several young people sitting in church depressed, and counselling has been delayed or not instituted.

The Barna Group article "*Three Spiritual Journeys of Millennials*," written on June 3, 2013, relates to the book *You Lost Me* by David Kinnaman (2011). In the book, Kinnaman divided the young people he surveyed into three groups: two groups have left the church and one had not. He called them Nomads, Prodigals, and Exiles. The survey revealed 43%, some 8 million youths, known as millennials, eighteen to twenty-nine years old had "dropped-off…who were once active churchgoers but who will no longer be particularly engaged in a church by their 30th birthday" according to the poll.

These young people have their own beliefs regarding Christianity, and it is contrary to traditional biblical doctrine. The Nomads believe that they are still Christians even though they do not attend church. They say that they have faith but not necessarily in God or the church. The Prodigals are those who have walked away from Christianity. They said that their experiences in the churches were bad, and they probably will not come back to the Christian faith. On the other hand, the Exiles are different from the Nomads and the Prodigals. They have not physically left the churches. But spiritually, they have challenges applying and complying with the teachings of the church as it relates to them personally. Some "32% say they want to be a Christian without separating themselves from the world around them" (Barna Group 2013).

This article provides a clear picture of the confused and bewildered mindset of the youth in and out of the church today. It touches on many of the concerns that this researcher is striving to uncover, one why young people are leaving the church and two what could potentially happen to the churches if all the young people are gone?

In another article by the Barna Group, "*What Young Adults Say Is Missing from Church*," written on November 13, 2019, a group of fifteen thousand or so young people, ages eighteen to thirty-five years old from twenty-five countries responded to the survey. It was posted online for two and a half months. Some six out of ten Christians pointed out that going to church, learning about God, and participating in the services helped them to grow spiritually. While others stated that the church had faults in its teachings. And as far as they were concerned, they did not need to learn anything else from the church for the time being (Barna 2019). At the top of the list of what is missing from church, 18% of the young people surveyed said that their friends were missing at church and social connections with other Christians (Barna 2019). Most of the people that come to church do not come just for the Word, but they come because they have connections/fellowships with each other. Camaraderie and friendly fellowship are essential to holding relationships and the church together as mentioned in Hebrews 10:25 (KJV).

Gallup: US Church Membership Down Sharply

Jeffrey M. Jones wrote "*U.S. Church Membership Down Sharply in Past Two Decades,*" published on April 18, 2019. In this article, Jones recorded that membership in synagogues, as well as churches, was down 50% in 2018. This percentage is the lowest it has been in the past twenty years. There has been an increase in the number of Americans who claim to have no religious affiliation (Jones 2019, 1–12). The study indicated, however, "At the turn of the century, 73% of U.S. adults with a religious preference belonged to a church, compared with 64% today" and the percentage continues to decline. The deceleration of adults belonging to a church or synagogue is an intergenerational disconnect. There is less engagement today between older adults, the "traditionalists, baby boomers, millennials and Generation X" than what it used to be twenty-some years ago. The article implied that the church leaders will need to provide opportunities to keep the young people interested and actively involved in the church ministries. And to aid in the growth of the church, young people will need encouragement to produce children and bring their families to church so that the apostolic teaching will continue.

Gallup: Why Are Americans Losing Confidence

"Why Are Americans Losing Confidence in Organized Religion?" is an article by Frank Newport, written on July 16, 2019.

The writer explained a continual and steady decline in the distrust of Americans for organized religion. The general sentiments of the population surveyed related to several horrific reports of immorality and hypocrisy among the church leaders and the church's refusal to embrace the LGBTQ (lesbian, gay, bisexual, transexual, queer) community who are hiding in the church. This article reported serious stories of allegations against clerics and administrators who held positions of authority and power in the church. Their shameful actions broke the people's trust and contributed to young people leaving the church.

Lifeway Research: Most Teenagers Drop Out of Church

According to an article by Aaron Earls entitled "Most Teenagers Drop Out of Church as Young Adults," written on January 15, 2019, interviewed Protestant Christians aged twenty-three to thirty said that they attended church two times a month or more when they were in high school, but they do not attend church anymore because of "a change in their life situation." As these young people experienced more autonomy, such as getting a driver's license, having employment, or moving away from home to attend college, 96% of them said these things led them away from the church; but they did not plan on leaving. The author stated that at the time of the survey. Among those in this study who had dropped out of church for a year, 31% of them had returned. But they said that they only want a "small dose of church" (Earls 2019).

It was unclear if the researcher's focus had included young adults who had quit attending church before or during college. Nevertheless, it was clear that young adults are leaving the church at a higher number than any other age group. We are losing a generation of churchgoers and this study seeks to find out and understand why.

Why Men Hate Going to Church

David Murrow, the author of *Why Men Hate Going To Church* (2005), uncovers some very revealing, surprising, and awkward reasons why men hate going to church from men he surveyed and observed. Murrow has gathered a lot of information as a churchgoing man with a history of attending several types of religious congregations over the years. Murrow stated in the introduction, "I am not a theologian, pastor or professor. I'm a man in the pews who, like so many others, has struggled to find his place in the church." This book provides many perspectives, problems, and issues experienced or felt by single and married men who had attended religious services sometime in their lives.

The author stated that a leading contributing factor that men gave for not attending church was that they look at church as a women's club, a place for women, children, and older men. Churches have more women than men in them, 65% of the churches in American are populated with women and one-fifth of the married women in the churches are sitting on pews without their husbands being with them. Men are absent from most Christian churches because they are bored in the worship service, uncomfortable in the environment, or just passive to keep their wives or mothers from nagging them about attending church. The landscape of the churches consists scarcely of men who are eighteen to thirty-five years old. Programs and activities designed by the church fit the needs and likes of women and children; planning and execution of programs have basically excluded things that interest men. Many leadership positions oftentimes are occupied by women in the church except for the office of pastor or bishop. Volunteerism is usually comprised of women due to the low attendance and participation from men. Murrow stated female participation in churches is evident more so in small churches or those churches with one hundred or less members.

In Murrow's book, Russell Rainey asked several men why they did not go to church anymore, and their answer was "There's nothing for me to do" (Murrow 2005). The author included comments from two celebrity ministers in his book. John Gray warns, "Not to be needed is slow death for a man," and Al Winsemann wrote that "deploying people in their areas of giftedness changes lives" (Murrow 2005). It is a matter of fact, not discrimination, but due to a lack of men in the church, women have had to fill in the gaps and maintained the functionality of the church. What may have been considered oversight or intentional was not meant to exclude men from having roles or performing tasks. If men attending the church, unlike those surveyed by Murrow, would acknowledge that they are interested and available to participate in the programming, operation, and management of the church, it is believed that they would be offered or assigned tasks and roles according to their qualifications without hesitation from those in authority.

The author stated that his study showed that churches tend to attract men who are passive, docile, meek, soft, or bookworms, which are descriptions of a "feminine attitude." Most masculine men are not interested in a feminine image of Jesus Christ. They do not want to be in an environment where Jesus Christ is referred to as sweet, compassionate, and a lover. Men follow men. When they come to church, they expect to be inspired by teachings and sermons about a strong, powerful, mighty, and courageous savior not a wimp. Murrow stated that this could be one of the reasons that gay men attend church and lesbian women keep away from church (Murrow 2005).

The author explained that single men from ages eighteen to thirty-five often prefer attending a large church with many congregants so that they are not targeted or pestered for not being married, and neither are they deceitfully set up with single women who are looking for a husband. Single men stated that they feel pressured in small churches to get married. So many are hiding out in megachurches where they can have several girlfriends and premarital sex without being judged.

Some other reasons expressed by the author why men are not attending church were reports of scandals in the news media about sexually abused children by male clerics in the churches. Some fathers interviewed exclaimed that they are afraid for their son's well-being, so they do not encourage them to go to church (Murrow 2005). Men grumbled that they hate it when worship services and preaching is to long as well as when the services are late starting. Women usually do not mind long services or services starting late because their attention span is longer than men. Men have also reported that they do not recall anything the teacher or preacher said because they talked too long. Murrow (2005) declared that there is a lot of teaching going on in church but not much listening. Howbeit, the teachers and preachers are not focused on a specific message or topic but jumping randomly across many things. It brings about confusion and people stop listening.

Murrow discussed recommendations that churches can adopt if they want to increase the growth of their local churches and the kingdom of God with men. He stated that churches could move their worship services to outside the church building. The services could be held in a parking lot, in a mall, in a school gymnasium, or in a hotel. It could attract men who do not want to come inside a church, it would be an invitation to be a part of the service. Worship service music that sounds like bedroom music can be a turnoff to men. The author stated, "Remember you are leading the people into battle not the bedroom" (Murrow 2005). Some of the men stated that they hated church décor that looked feminine. It was suggested that the church environment or walls should not look like a flower garden or be painted in soft colors like pink and lavender. Preachers, evangelists, ministers, and altar workers should avoid rushing to lay their hands on people. Visiting men stated that they were uncomfortable getting in the prayer lines at the church because there were to many people touching all over their bodies. The prayer at the altar should be kept short and to the point (Murrow 2005).

This book *Why Men Hate Going To Church* was a trailblazer for other authors of religious literature, investigative reporting, and statisticians who present data on the population and geographics relating to Christianity. The information, interviews, and data incorporated in Murrow's book is a profound wake-up call to church leadership, the laity, and especially the women who have for years operated and functioned in an unchanging manner as the number of men dwindled down to almost zero in several churches. Traditionally, churches have maintained the same status quo from one generation to the next generation without effectively reaching a broader base of young people and men as new members in the church.

The author explored meaningful patterns and processes that can be implemented and expanded in ways that will be beneficial to the current culture and climate of the Christian faith. Murrow boldly opened up and shined light on so many dark corners and facets of our churchgoing experiences that had never honestly been acknowledged before now. His book has left an indelible imprint on this researcher's mindset. The researcher believe that this is a transformative moment for our churches as we strive to develop physical and spiritual growth. It is time for our Pentecostal Apostolic churches to step outside the walls of the buildings and do as Jesus said, "Follow me, and I will make you fishers of men" (Matthew 4:19 KJV). We must go out of our comfort zones sometimes to reach young people and men for Christ's sake.

Why Are the Young People Leaving the Church? What We Need to Do to Keep Them In

The author Ruben Joseph presents a down to earth easy to read book on his interviews with those who were associated with him in ministry. He writes about those who are attending church and those who have left the church. He gives suggestions on what the church can do to keep young people in the church. Joseph makes it clear that he is actively involved with young people. He is an Haitian preacher in a Seventh-Day Adventist Church.

Why Are the Young People Leaving The Church? What We Need to Do to Keep Them In (2011) is a concise literary work that examines the attractions and trickery of Satan along with man-made traditions. He points out that Satan's devices have encapsulated and devoured churchgoers. He writes how old cultures and man-made traditions have hindered many young people from joining the church as well as remaining in the churches. Ruben Joseph purposefully imparts specific scriptural texts to match whatever issue he is writing about in the book. He also gives short stories of what is happening in the churches to the young people and their reactions. Joseph teaches and preaches that he finds that the young people are becoming too closely familiar and comfortable around worldliness. And it is capturing them physically, emotionally, and spiritually. As a result, young people are confused and mixed up on what to believe and who to believe.

Therefore, they are relying on their own fleshly desires without consideration of the consequences for their ungodly actions.

According to the author, some young people are unhappy attending church because they think that they are missing out on fun in the world. They fail to realize and understand that Christians have fun in church while engaging in morally clean activities such as sports, drama, Christian parties, et cetera. The difference between having godly fun and having fun in the world is that people do not wake up with shame, regrets, hangovers, or having to deal with consequences from bad choices. Worshipping and praising God in church is fun. The spirit produces joy.

Some youth reported that leaders of the church especially preachers publicly expose the sins of young people out in the open by calling them out or using their names in the sermons. He stated that adults who are known to have committed sins are quietly reprimanded behind closed doors instead of being publicly humiliated like the youths. When young people are embarrassed in the church, they are less likely to ever return to Christian faith. Joseph (2011) points out, "A church without young people is a dead church."

Another observation from the author is that young people feel like they are overlooked or ignored by autocratic authorities in the church and their opinions are not valued. Young adults voiced that they are expected to carry on the work of the church in the future, but nobody is training them for the task. They are leaving the churches because of the elders or governing church body's resistance to modifications of any kind. Church members are from different cultures, and their beliefs vary, for instance, about wearing jewelry. For one culture in the church, it is compulsory for married individuals to wear wedding bands, and others are instructed not to wear them. Some wear decorative jewelry on their clothes or hair while some do not. Because elders are pervasively arguing over petty things like jewelry and clothing, young people are not tolerant over debates. They say that they do not see disagreement in the world like what they see in religious groups, so they choose to follow the world (Joseph 2011).

The author also stated that he met young people who no longing attend church because they said that their parents were phony and hypocrites. They act one way in church and act another way when they get home. Joseph declares that young children and adult children are looking for their parents to be genuine and truthful. Some of the young people complained about the preacher's ministry on prosperity. Young people reportedly said that the only ones they saw being prosperous were the preachers. The congregations never received any of the promised financial blessings predicted by the prophets and preachers. Prosperity ministry was a complete turnoff to young adults (Joseph 2011).

In the book, Joseph speaks to parents regarding the transition of their children living at home with supervision to living on college campus completely independent of parental guidance. Quite often, young people's minds are reshaped at college by teachers who are not Christians but atheists. Young people are faced with peer pressure to join fraternities or sororities. And some, for the first time, feel as though they can do whatever they want without being controlled by adults. So they go wild and usually get into dangerous situations. The author recommends that parents pray for their children daily; start to teach and encourage them to read the Bible. Teach them to ask God to help them to serve him before and while at college (Joseph 2011).

This book helps to explain some of the problems that young people are facing in the church and everyday life. It offers steadfast remedies according to the scriptures in the Word of God. It is important for young people to be baptized and filled with the Holy Ghost so that they will be spiritually fortified to overcome and fight the enemy of their soul through Jesus Christ.

Youth Leaving the Church? How to Reverse This Trend

Dr. Joyce T. Henderson (2001), the author of *Youth Leaving the Church? How To Reverse This Trend,* is an experienced certified marriage and family counselor. She has pastored several churches in the California region. Dr. Henderson said she cited in her book reasons young people reported to her in group meetings and other occasions for them leaving the churches. Some teenagers and young adults said that they were not recognized or appreciated for the work that they had done at their churches. Some of the members of the churches were aggressive toward them, and they disrespected their privacy and independence. Some were baptized to please their family members or to have a romantic relationship with the opposite sex at the church, but they were not fully committed to being saved. Some felt that the church members were a parade of hypocrites and self-righteous people. Young people reported, "Bishops and other leaders remain isolated and do not visit with them. They sometimes wonder do they really care or even know them" (Henderson 2001).

The author stated that parents bear some responsibility for the youth leaving the church. Henderson stated that parents of young children bring toys or electronic devices for their child to play with while worship services are going on. From an early age to their teenage years, these children developed a practice of playing in church so for many they continue to play in church as adults. Because they learned at a young age that they can be entertained, or they could entertain themselves in church. Young people and adults are seen today in church entertaining themselves with playing games or texting their friends on their cell phones while service is going on, at a time when they should be listening, learning, and engaging in the worship to almighty God. They are missing out on hearing and learning the Word of God and developing a spiritual relationship with Jesus Christ.

We have all seen parents take their children and go sit on the back pew to keep them quiet, and they give them toys to play with. Instead of the parents teaching them to sit still and encourage them to participate in the services. Though these children may have been raised in church, they have not really heard the Word of God because they were playing. This author took a quote from another author named John Flavel. He said, "If you neglect to instruct your children in the way of holiness, will the devil neglect to instruct them in the way of wickedness? No, if you will not teach them to pray, Satan will teach them to lie and curse. If ground is uncultivated, weeds will grow" (Henderson 2001).

As we have observed, there are many young and older adults sitting in church today, and they are still playing in church. They come to church to be entertained by the music and activities without being converted by the unadulterated word. Since they are void of the word and knowledge of God, they cannot instruct their children. According to Dr. Henderson, children's first and best teachers are their parents. From parents, children learn how to be faithful, committed, and consistent with their walk following Christ or else they learn how to pretend to be a Christian. Henderson uses a term for fake Christians; she called them "plastic Christian" because they are not real Christians. The author documented statistics showing where both parents are faithful to the Lord and "actively work in the congregation that 93% of the kids remained faithful. If only one of the parents were faithful, the figure dropped to 73%. In homes where only one of the parents attended and only mildly active in the work of the ministry, only 53% of the children stay faithful…in cases where both parents attended only infrequently, the percentage of the children who remained faithful plummeted to a woeful 6%" (Henderson 2001). As children grow into adulthood, they usually will do what they have seen their parents do for many generations.

Henderson described some of the same reasons in her book for young people leaving the churches like many of those already documented by previous researchers. However, she does point out some different reasons that others did not write about. She wrote that teens and young adults, eighteen to twenty-five years old, are being persuaded to leave the Christian faith by cults. Cults are referred to in her writing as spiritually "abusive churches." Because they lead the congregation by control, submissive manipulation, rigid lifestyle, intimidation, and brainwashing (Henderson 2001). These organized religious entities are labeled churches. Several of them are like mainstream denominations but with a different "twist," some claim to follow Christ and others have their own human deity who say that they have had a revelation from God. Cults strategically and intentionally target teenagers and young adults who are seen as being alone, dissatisfied with their family life or religious beliefs, immature, or confused about how to handle day-to-day life circumstances.

Dr. Henderson proposes the following for reasons that young people are attracted to cults:

1. Their protest against social injustices.
2. Their agenda to improve the world.
3. Their provisions and a place to live.
4. Their encouragement of personal development for members.
5. Their agenda to provide a finer, purer, physical, and moral environment.
6. Their agenda on lessons of cultural differences.
7. Their agenda to provide an alternative to employment and dead-end jobs (Henderson 2001).

Dr. Henderson warns parents and church leaders to be on guard for cults who are trying to recruit young people such as "Mormons, Jehovah's Witnesses, Christian Science, The Way International, and the Unity School of Christianity" (Henderson 2001). She said that they reach out to the youth as caring individuals and groups to win the confidence of unsuspecting teens and young adults. Because so many children and young people feel that their families and church family do not care about them, these cults express words of comfort through distribution of false doctrines and literature. They pose as educators teaching classes at community colleges, and they make arrangement for the vulnerable to have face-to-face meetings with adults to supposedly guide and counsel them in making the right decisions. Oftentimes, they give youths the attention that they are seeking under a cloak of disguise, deceit, and secrecy. These organizations and hierarchical church leaders are charlatans that Apostle Paul warned Timothy and the church about in 1 Timothy 4:1–4 (KJV).

The author set forth strongly the need for teenagers and young people to be taught the Word of God from the Bible so that they will be able to defend the gospel of Jesus Christ and be prepared to distinguish truth from the lies of Satan. Parents and church leaders also need to be familiar with the teachings and philosophies of existing cults so that they can be easily recognized to prevent our families and friends from becoming prey to them. It is necessary for young people everywhere to study and understand the Word of God and be trained in discipleship and how to evangelize in this world. Dr. Henderson gave a lot of information in a few words surrounding the problems and causes of our young people leaving the church. She offered a tradition that we all can fall back on and that is prayer. Prayer works; it is a proven fact. Prayer is what the churches need to do more of as intercessors for our current and future generations to grow our churches and sustain our Christian faith.

Will Our Children Have Faith?

John H. Westerhoff III (2012), writer of the book *Will Our children Have Faith*, proposed a particular unique method for teaching children Christian education. It was not readily accepted by several churches and schools of thought forty to fifty years ago. Dr. Westerhoff provided a picturesque description of his career from teaching at Harvard University, on board as a faculty member at Duke University Divinity School for Christian education. He travelled all over the world participating in multiple religious academia arenas teaching, asking questions, and interviewing scholars from different denominations to becoming a priest, a pastor, a teacher, and an author of articles and books on religion. He stated in this book that he is a "professional church educator" (Westerhoff III 2012).

Dr. Westerhoff wrote this book in 1976 and has since made revisions by popular demands of laities and church leaders to keep the book in circulation and print. This researcher has the third revision on hand that was written in 2012. According to Westerhoff, schooling-instructional paradigm is not effective in teaching children or adults specific matter. The following is the schooling-instructional paradigm explanation in Aurora Institute:

> The instructional paradigm, still in place in
> most schools, was primarily designed to support
> the function of teaching, or more specifically, the
> delivery of information from instructor to stu-

dent.... More than a century of experience with instruction-driven design has proven that teaching does not always equal learning.

The author argued that Christian education or Sunday school ministry is lacking in transmitting important religious and spiritual instructions because the teachers are spewing out instructions to the students without interactions from them. Basically, the attendees or students are hearing the teacher but not necessarily listening to apply what is being taught; therefore, such information is easily forgotten. Westerhoff proposes that churches, institutions, and Sunday schools change their method of teaching to enculturation. Enculturation is the process or way that members of a community learn the culture of the group or family by observation, experience, and instructions.

It is in the "interaction between and among us" that children, youth, and adults learn and hold on to the information and instructions that they have received in the process of learning. Dr. Westerhoff emphasized that we learn by doing as well as stay in the church by participating (Westerhoff III 2012). He said, for a lesson on buying groceries, we watched our parents buy the grocery, we learned how to buy food. So the same learning process occurs in our churches when we include children, youth, and adults in all the church rituals. The author mentioned that not everyone is able to understand and remember context through instructional learning, where the teacher teaches, and the student is expected to learn. Over the years, public schools, private schools, and seminaries have changed, recognized, and accepted that people learn in different styles and ways. Some learners prefer learning visually, auditory, reading/writing, and kinesthetic or hands-on.

Dr. Westerhoff believes that changing Christian education and Sunday school curriculums to enculturation/interactive learning, which focuses on student learning and participation is the most effective way to teach the youth and young adults about the Lord Jesus Christ. The author stated, "Our children will have faith if we have faith and are faithful. Both we and our children will have Christian faith if we join with others in a worshiping, learning, witnessing Christian community of faith" (Westerhoff III 2012).

This researcher agrees with the author that enculturation or interactive instructional model is necessary for the growth of the church now and in the future. There are many gifted, talented, and intelligent young people in the church who are weary of coming to church and not learning anything or not being asked to participate in the worship services and other activities scheduled or plan for the congregation. Because they are bored, they lose interest in coming to church and find other things to do out there in the world. Though, Dr. Westerhoff's explanations and recommendations were geared toward the Episcopal Church. The above method of teaching is pertinent in the Pentecostal Apostolic churches for this new age of technical learning and sustainability of young people in the Lord's church.

Love Is The Way: Holding on to Hope in Troubling Times

The book *Love Is The Way: Holding on to Hope in Troubling Times*, written by Bishop Michael Curry with Sara Grace (2020), brings to the forefront some difficult topics regarding current and past issues on racism, social, health, education, and economical disparity among American churches and communities. Bishop Curry makes it known that he is the presiding bishop of the Episcopal Church, a priest, a pastor, and a spiritual and political advocate for those who are mistreated, misunderstood, oppressed, and in need of love. He is and has been associated with many renowned history makers such as Dr. M. L. King, archbishop of Canterbury; former president Bill Clinton; and author Maya Angelo. He rallied for socioeconomic changes relating to the water issues in Flint, Michigan, and the Sioux tribe at Standing Rock in North Dakota. He is well acquainted with the struggles of inequality. He challenges leaders to join the fight for the purposes of transforming people, legislation, and communities through love.

The author believes that love—that is, agape love—the love of God displayed toward and among people in the church and community as well as those serving in government administrations will improve the well-being of the present generation and future generations. So many young people have turned away from the church to serve themselves. He said, "We've got a whole generation of kids who are now growing into adulthood, whose only rituals and commandments are those of the streets" (Curry 2020). Bishop Curry provided many stories of failure turned into stories of triumph through the power of love. Love is one of the keys in closing the gap between this generation and the next generation without comprising the standards justice or holiness.

Chapter 2

Early Church History

Between the book of Malachi in the Old Testament and the book of Matthew in the New Testament, there exist a period of four hundred years; it is referred to as "The Inter-Testament Period, Four Hundred Silent Years" (Stringfellow 2014).

During this time, there was no recorded interaction between God and man. God did not speak to Israel. There was no record of new prophets called or documentation of new events pertaining to the nation of Israel because the Jewish people ignored the tenets of the Old Testament. Many of the Israelites outwardly and spiritually rebelled against God. They lacked repentance. They failed to adhere to the commandments of Jehovah God. We do not hear of God speaking to mankind again until we open and read the first pages in the New Testament of Matthew.

The book of Matthew introduces humanity to the savior of the world Jesus by a genealogy list of forty-two patriarchs. This prophetic message is about the one that the Jewish people had been waiting for many years the Messiah, Jesus Christ, the anointed one, the son of God. Jesus Christ was the fulfillment of the Old Testament prophecies. The four gospels Matthew, Mark, Luke, and John provides us with a panoramic view of the life of Jesus from his birth to his activities as a youth, to his baptism, his choosing of twelve disciples, his teaching and preaching and many accounts of him performing amazing miracles and wonderments up to the moment of his death.

We see Jesus as a thirty-year-old being baptized by John the Baptist, and afterward, he began his earthly ministry. He journeyed on the roads to Galilee, Jerusalem, Judea, Samaria, and other regions in the Roman Empire. He was teaching and preaching righteousness, and the kingdom of heaven "from that time Jesus began to preach, and to say, Repent: for the kingdom of heaven is at hand" (Matthew 4:17 KJV). He performed miracles, healed varies types of diseases and sicknesses, cast out devils, discerned the wicked hearts of the Pharisees and Sadducees and triumphed over sin and Satan during his three and one-half years of ministering. Nearing the end, Jesus was publicly criticized and falsely accused by the ruling Jewish leaders. He was scourged and sentenced to death under the Roman authority of Pontius Pilate. He was crucified on Calvary's cross as a substitutionary sacrificial lamb for the sins of the entire world. He was buried in the borrowed tomb of Joseph of Arimathea. Gloriously on the third day, he rose from the grave with all power in his hands as the scriptures declared in the synoptic gospels of Matthew, Mark, Luke, and John.

Jesus being God incarnate, conquered death, hell, and the grave. It is important to acknowledge that Jesus Christ did something that no other human being could do. He was the only man of flesh who died, was buried, and rose from the dead, never to die again. He lives forevermore. Jesus, the son of God has two natures: he is both human (fleshy) and divine (spirit). He came purposely from heaven to earth to die for our sins. His precious blood paid the redemptive price for the sins of the whole world, and he reconciled us back to himself. Jesus Christ is the savior of the world. Salvation was made available to the Jews first and then to the Gentiles, and to whosoever believe in him for redemption and salvation through his shed blood. John 3:16 (KJV) says, "For God so loved the world, that he gave his only begotten Son, that whosoever believeth in him should not perish, but have everlasting life."

The Pentecostal Apostolic Church is Christ centered on the death, burial, resurrection, faith, and teachings of Jesus Christ and the apostles. The doctrine of Jesus Christ is the oneness of God, it is monotheistic as outline in Deuteronomy 6:4 (KJV), "Hear, O Israel:

The Lord our God is one Lord." It is not established in Trinitarian or Christian science or any other tradition or doxology. But predicated on the belief in one deity, one God above all gods. It is not shared or intertwined with the worship of Buddhism, Hinduism, Jainism, Taoism, Catholicism, or any other god.

According to 1 Corinthians 15:5–6 (KJV), Jesus was distinctly and uniquely different from the realities commonly known physiologically to mankind in that he was pronounced dead, but he came back to life on the third day. The proof of his miraculous and glorious resurrection was witnessed by Cephas (Peter), the twelve apostles, and the women who supported his ministry such as Mary Magdalene, Joanna, and Susanna. Sometime after Jesus's resurrection, approximately five hundred tombs were opened. Dead people rose from their sleep of death, and they were seen alive in Jerusalem by people who knew that they had been dead (Matthew 27:52 KJV). In Jesus's discourse with the apostles and disciples, he foretold of his impending death and the significance of his resurrection. But many did not believe what he preached or taught, including some of the disciples and members of his own family. However, to their astonishment, Jesus appeared to them as he had said and instructed them to go and meet him in Jerusalem, for there he would send the Comforter, his spirit.

Prior to his ascension, Jesus was with the apostles for forty days after his resurrection; it was the end of the Jewish celebration of the Passover, and the celebration of the Festival of Weeks known as Shavuot in Hebrew and Pentecost in Greek reference from Russell and Wall (2004). At the end of the forty days, our blessed savior was taken up into heaven while the disciples watched him ascend into the clouds where he is now seated on the right hand of the throne of God (Luke 16:19). With the faith of the disciples intact, they travel to Jerusalem as commanded by Jesus Christ to await the promise of the Comforter, the Holy Ghost.

Ten days after Jesus's departure, the 120 disciples all assembled in an upper room in Jerusalem waited for the promise of the Holy Ghost, that is, the Comforter. A quote from David K. Bernard denotes that "The Holy Ghost is our Comforter" (John 14:26),

"Greek (parakletos) yet God the Father is the God of all comfort (paraklesis) who comforts (parakaleo) us in all our tribulation" (Bernard 2001).

Now, when the Israelites had given their first fruit grain offerings and meat offerings, Pentecost was completed as stated in Acts 2. Pentecost (Shavuot) was accomplished on the fiftieth day after Passover. Pentecost was only one day. At the climax of the Festival of Weeks celebration (first fruit grain harvest), the spirit of God entered the room where the 120 believers were gathered. The transforming spirit and power of the Holy Ghost described in Acts 2:1–4 manifested itself like, "a sound from heaven as a rushing mighty wind and it filled the house…there appeared unto them cloven tongues like as of fire…and they were all filled with the Holy Ghost and began to speak in other tongues."

The Day of Pentecost was the beginning of the New Testament Church and the establishment of Christianity. *Wycliffe Bible Dictionary* defines the word *church* translated "the Gr. ekklesia which never refers to a place of worship but has in view an assembly of people…a local company of believers" (Pfeiffer, Vos, Rea 1999). The definition of Christianity as "the religion founded by Jesus Christ. Following His ascension, the apostles in the power of the Holy Spirit preached in His name. They taught that He was God's Son, the Messiah; they gathered a community of believers; and they exhorted all to a holy life" (Pfeiffer, Vos, Rea 1999). The New Testament Church began on AD 33 in Jerusalem (Acts 2:1–4, 36, 38 KJV).

When Jesus died on Calvary's cross for the sins of the world, the Jewish temple veil (representing his body) was torn in two parts. It was symbolic of the way into the holy of holies, the entrance of salvation was opened to all people. So the Jews as well as the nation of Gentiles can have access to God incarnate in Jesus Christ (Matthew 27:50–51 KJV). The New Testament Church originated from the preaching and teaching of Jesus and the twelve apostles. Jesus Christ is the founder, high priest, and chief cornerstone of the Pentecostal Apostolic Church and not the pope. The scripture text recorded in Hebrews 4:14–16 (NIV) confirms: "Therefore, since we have a great high priest who has ascended into heaven, Jesus the Son of God, let us hold firmly to the faith we profess." The New Testament Church is built on Jesus Christ not Peter, and it belongs to Jesus. Jesus said that he purchased the church with his own blood and that it is built upon him, and the gates of hell will not destroy it (Acts 20:28, 16:13–20 KJV).

On the day of Pentecost, the 120 Galileans disciples were heard speaking in tongues as the spirit of God gave them the ability to speak. They spoke in unknown tongues as well as languages familiar to the seventeen nations of "devout men, out of every nation" who were there in Jerusalem (Acts 2:5–6 KJV). As the anointing of the Holy Ghost directed Peter, he preached Jesus to them beginning from the Old Testament regarding the prophesies by the prophet Joel and King David to the crucifixion and ascension of Jesus Christ. That day, three thousand believers, along with the 120 were born again and added to the church (Acts 2:1–41 KJV). The Christians were unified with one mind and one purpose to support and grow the new church. They demonstrated acts of charity and kindness as they shared what they had with each other in the community of believers. Daily God added more converts to the church as the apostles boldly preached the gospel, the good news of Jesus Christ (Acts 11:26 KJV).

Persecution and Breakaway from New Testament Church

The upper room disciples and the new born again believers of the New Testament Church like the founding fathers of America in 1776 were energetic and fearless in their pursuit to transform the lives of many as they carried the Word of God enjoined with the Great Commission of Matthew 28:19. The apostles journeyed from Jerusalem to all parts of the earth preaching the gospel, teaching, baptizing converts in the name of Jesus Christ. They healed all kinds of diseases and set souls free from demonic spirits by the power of the Holy Ghost. And people became disciples as the Christian church grew.

The apostles were faithful believers who became missionaries and servants of Jesus Christ in changing the world through the Word of God. As the Holy Ghost led them to spread the gospel, they faced many challenges, dangers, hostility, opposition, rejection, and death threats from Jewish leaders: priests, scribes, Pharisees, Sadducees, Sanhedrin, and Roman authorities. They continued proclaiming the truth of salvation with fervent prayer and fasting. Terror and fear invaded the assemblies of the saints. Soon they were persecuted for preaching and healing in the name of Jesus. These dedicated brethren suffered beatings, stoning, imprisonment, being cast into lions' dens, burned at the stake, and varies martyrdoms. Nevertheless, without hesitation they sacrificed their freedom and lives as they carried the gospel throughout Jerusalem, Judea, Samaria, and the world.

In the Book of Acts chapter 7 records Stephen's first martyrdom death by stoning, followed by Apostle James's execution with a sword in chapter 12. Tragically, many of the apostles died horrific deaths, but the accounts of their deaths are not all detailed in the Bible. However, they are preserved in the manuscripts of ancient Jewish historian such as Flavius Josephus and historian of Christianity Eusebius of Caesarea, also known as Eusebius Pamphili. The apostle Paul (formerly known as Saul) waged a brutal campaign against the saints to destroy the newly formed religion instituted by Jesus Christ until one day on the road to Damascus Jesus revealed himself to him (Acts 9:1–9 KJV). After his conversion to Christianity, he dedicated the rest of his life preaching and teaching the gospel until he was executed by the Roman Emperor Nero 67 or 68 AD (Smith 1986).

As predicted by Apostle Paul, the Christian churches in Asia Minor and other countries were attacked by political authorities and previous religious church leaders. Timothy, the most famous protégé of Apostle Paul, was warned of the soon-to-be apostasy within the churches from false teachers and false preachers. They would attempt to subvert the gospel of Jesus Christ with their philosophies, pompous ideas, and irreverent interpretation of scriptures. Some would separate themselves from the true churches to forge new doctrines of devils being seduced by Satan (1 Timothy 4:1 KJV).

We have read in the scriptures where Apostle Peter, Apostle John, and Jude scholarly wrote letters to the churches to warn the church against destructive heresies and dissemination of false teachings. These false teachers and preachers materialized from within the churches. They practiced immortality and blatantly rejected the word of truth from God. These individuals sought to bring disorder and confusion and to change the mindset of the saints by reforming the doctrine that the apostles had labored so hard to deliver to the churches. Several of these false teachers and false preachers exploited the church to promote their own personal agendas (2 Peter 2:1–3 KJV). Outside of the church, a larger enemy appeared, the Romans, who anticipated and planned to shut down the church. They hated this new religion of Jewish Christians called "The Way" (Acts 9:2 and 19:9 KJV). Despite great persecution the early church had hope. The letters from the apostles encouraged them to hold on to their faith in Jesus Christ who will one day reward them.

Violence and threat of violence continued during the early church from the time of the apostles through to the demise of the Roman Empire. According to *The Everything Christianity Book* by Michael F. Russell and Amy Wall (2004), when Rome burned in AD 64, Nero who was the emperor at that time accused the Christians of setting Rome on fire. He blamed them to cover up his crime. It is around this event that it is believed that Nero murdered Apostles Paul and Peter along with countless Christians. Documented in history is the worst persecution of the early church. It occurred during the wick evil reign of Emperor Decius in AD 250. The Romans demanded that the Christians offer sacrifice to their pagan gods and worship Emperor Caesar as god. When the Christians refused to bow down, they were tortured to death.

Decius believed that if he burnt the scriptures, then Christianity would be abolished. The scriptures were burned but Christianity remained through oral recitations. The saints had learned the scriptures and were well versed in them. Whatever letters survived from the apostles were shared from one congregation to another congregation. The unsightly persecution of the early church believers continued up until the deaths of Emperor Decius in AD 305 and Emperor Diocletian about AD 312 (Russell and Wall 2004). All praise and glory go to the faith, perseverance, and bravery of the martyred saints. Thank the Lord Jesus Christ for the sustainability of his holy Word despite the many attempts to destroy it and the believers.

Treatment of Children in Jesus's Time

The ancient meaning of the word *family* in Aramaic and in Hebrew held a wide variety of usage to include one's husband, wife, brothers, sisters, half-brothers, half-sisters, sons, daughters, cousins, and extended family members. It was essential to have recognizable connectivity to family for protection and survival in those days. Oftentimes, married couples with their children lived in the same house as the grandparents or in the same village as their relatives. The eldest, generally the father of the clan or tribe, was considered the head of the household with full authority to govern and make decisions that affected the entire family structure. The patriarch had the power to put a family member to death or sell the children in the family into slavery without repercussions. Children had little to no value or voice in the family. They were expected to work. Agriculturally, they planted and harvested the food. They took care of the herds of animals. Their family's survival depended on their hard work inside and outside the home.

Prior to Christianity, according to Jennifer Haddad Mosher's article *"Then and Now: Early Christianity's Radical Reshaping of Childhood"* (2017), children in Roman societies were not valued or thought of as a human being like grown-ups. Their status was just a cut above cattle, they were considered property. It was at birth that the Roman father would decide if the child would live or die. Unwanted or ill children were "smothered, or abandoned to die by exposure, succumbing to the elements or wild animals" (Mosher 2017). Some children escaped death if they were abandoned and rescued by neighbors who raised them as orphans or held on to them as slaves. Legally, parents had the right to beat, kill, or sell their children without fear of punishment from the law. Many children did not live to reach puberty or become young adults. However, the teaching and preaching of Jesus and his example of treatment toward children gradually caught on within the religious territories. The following is a quote from Mosher, "Christians began to diverge from their neighbors and believe that children were person, inherently valuable, as adults. And, over time, that belief grew strong enough that they were willing to defy local customs …teaching against abortifacients and infanticide" (Mosher 2017). Abortifacients were herbs and drugs used to induce abortions whereas infanticide was the killing of infants within the first year of life (*Merriam-Webster Dictionary*).

Matthew 19:13 (KJV) demonstrated Jesus's love for children when parents brought their little children to him. He put his hands on them and prayed for them.

The disciples objected to the interruption by parents with their children. Jesus had been teaching the multitudes and his critics, the Pharisees, a lesson on marriage and divorce. Jesus acknowledged the presence of the little children. Despite opposition from his disciples, he granted the parents' request for their children to be blessed by him. Only he could know what lay ahead in the future of those children, so he prayed over them. Jesus illustrated the importance of the life and well-being of children and the parents' responsibility and obligation to bring them to Him. Jesus loves little children because they are innocent with humble, sweet spirits. Children are usually quite agreeable in most situations. In fact, Jesus specified that except adults exhibit faith and submission to him as children, they cannot go to heaven.

The New Testament provides evidence of Jesus concern and mercy for children in its stories about them. We can read where Jesus miraculously healed and raised Jairus's twelve-year-old daughter from the dead (Mark 5:21–24, 35–44 KJV). On another occasion, Jesus walked by a funeral procession, reached out his hand and touched the coffin of a dead young man. At the touch of Jesus, the only child of the widow of Nain supernaturally came to life and spoke to his mother (Luke 7:11–15 KJV). Remarkably, the Canaanite woman pleaded with Jesus to exorcise the demon out of her daughter. Though the custom and divinely appointed time of the Gentiles had not come yet, this Gentile woman approached Jesus in faith. She believed with her whole heart that he would heal her child. Jesus healed the child because of the mother's faith.

Children are important to Jesus (Matthew 15:21–28 KJV). Just like Jesus was concerned and cared about children in the days of the Bible, his love continues in these modern days as well. The early church grew out of love and compassion for each other and the unchurched. Leadership in the churches today must show love and concern to the young people by incorporating their ideas, experiences, and twenty-first-century technology. Many young people are looking for attention, love, and compassion; they want to be included and share their experiences with adults. It will strengthen relations between the ages, grow, expand, and secure the integrity of the future church of millennials and generation Z. The Bible states that children are a gift from God and that grandchildren are a crown to the elderly and glory to their parents, but this can only be fulfilled when parents, grandparents, and mature adults spend time and energy training their off springs in the ways of the Lord (Psalm 127:3; Proverbs 17:6 NLT). Older people are dying out, and it is important that children take an active part in the functionality of the church in these challenging times. Otherwise, when the elderly people die, many churches will close because the youth are unprepared to lead in the kingdom of God.

Christianity's Response to Mental Health Disorders in the Early Church and in the Present Day

In the early Christian era, it was not understood that the brain could get sick like the body could get sick. Tragically persons who were mentally ill suffered great pain, persecution, abuse, abandonment, and neglect at the hands of people in society and people in the church. Dr. Weiss's article, "Psychiatry's Ancient Origins," explained that in history, people called on "shamans, sorcerers, magicians, mystics, priests and other approved healers to treat illnesses" (2018). Sketched in the minds was the idea that if they would appease the gods of the land or complete some sacrificial ceremony requirements, then the person(s) would be healed, or the sickness would be prevented.

Members of the ancient Christian churches and societies thought that a person who displayed erratic behavior or emotional outbursts were possessed by a demon(s) and somehow sin was the cause of their acting out. The holy scriptures have supplied depictions of men and women in the Bible who may have had some sort of psychological condition from their belief in or indulgence in the occult, worship of idols, use of hallucinogenic, consumption of too much wine, or participation in sinful acts which could provide a portal for evil spirits to dwell in them. Jesus recognized the presence of the devil and his cohorts in them. With his great power and authority, he cast demons out of the people who were possessed. We see examples in the Gospels of demonic possession of people's bodies, minds, and spirits, which was exhibited in some physiological sign as a man could not talk, a man was blind, a boy had seizures, a man was insane, a Syrophoenician woman's daughter was healed of demonic possession and so on (Matthew 9:32–33, 12:22, 17:18; Mark 5:1–20, 7:24–30; Luke 4:33–36; Acts 16:16–18 NLT). Jesus, knowing all things, healed the body, mind, and spirit of those that came to him or were brought to him for healing and deliverance.

The early Christian churches and their medical community lacked scientific knowledge, early intervention, treatment, and medicine to treat and cure medical and psychological conditions affecting the brain. Since there was no treatment or cure for chemical and hormonal imbalances in the brain that caused unusual or bizarre behaviors in children and adults, many people suffered and died.

Nowadays, mental illness is more recognizable but not necessarily more accepted in societies, families, or churches. The Pentecostal Apostolic churches and more so the Afro-American churches need to step up to the plate and assist in the reformation processes on mental health disparity through proper education and training to tear down the stigmas surrounding mental illness in our churches, families, and communities. A preacher recently said that "depression is now called the common cold of mental illness" (David Jeremiah, *What Are You afraid of? Depression: The Fear of Mental Breakdown*; https://sermons.love). Depression is quite common among people in every walk of life today. The probability of someone in our churches and families with a mental health disorder is as common today as someone with diabetes and hypertension. We should respect mental ill as any other disease. Though improvements in early detection and screenings are available, there are still too many young and old Christians falling through the cracks when they could be receiving care. Our congregations must be educated on signs, symptoms of mental health disorders, and have access to affordable resources for care and treatment to preserve the health of our brethren. Geneva College, a Christian college, expounded on "The Stigma Around Mental Illness for Christians"; they said mental health education and training are necessary in keeping those with depression, anxiety, bipolar, schizophrenia, angry issues, post-traumatic stress disorder, and suicidal ideation included and supported in our churches, families, and societies. Because people are afraid of the unknown, they isolate themselves from people with mental illness. It is difficult for some to admit that they have mental health disorders or challenges to manage everyday activities. However, we, the church, ought to help those in need to maintain a sense of normalcy in their life.

Church people oftentimes are afraid that the conditions that those with behavior disorders have might jump off the person on to them. Not all mental health problems are of the devil. People should not have to suffer in silent. It is important that clerics preach and teach about mental health disorders as clearly recorded in the Bible and encourage the people of God to seek professional help from mental-health practitioners. Mental illness does not go away with prayer alone. Like those sick in the body have to schedule an appointment to see a doctor so should those mentally ill make an appointment and see a psychiatrist, psychologist, or Christian counselor. Jesus said, those that are well do not need a physician but those that are sick need a physician (Mark 2:17 KJV). Pastors, preachers, evangelists, officers of the church, young people, and adults are losing hope. Because they are exhausted, fatigued, frustrations, disappointments, distressed, weary, lonely, struggling financially, sick, bombarded with negative thoughts and weighted down with cares of life today. They believe and feel like nobody in the church cares about their problems or state of mind. It is vital that the body of believers express to those who are going through difficulties that they are not alone. Tell them that the church is with them and is available to assist them with whatever it is that they are going through. Encourage them to talk about their problem and trust in Jesus and get professional help.

Mental health disorders are not restricted to the laity, it encompasses humanity. The growth and strength of the church lies in its' transparency, and it starts with leadership. We all, bishops, pastors, ministers, missionaries, and members of the church have experienced mental health disturbances at some time or other another. Issues in life whether good or bad experiences should be shared with the saints and not kept secret. Mental illness is not a shame, it is a disease/disorder. Members of the body of Christ should be opened to share their testimonies about what they went through or are going through to help others who maybe going through the same problems or something similar. It exposes the vulnerability of leadership, and it validates that we are our brother's keeper. When teenagers, young adults, and mature adults hear that their leaders' testimonies, they recognize that they are not superhuman beings but regular people. People like them who encounter the same afflictions, diseases, troubles, and emotional breakdowns as everybody else. Verbalization of one's problems or weakness takes the power from the enemy. The Bible declares that it is by our testimonies that we overcome (Revelation 12:11 KJV). It enriches the fellowship and love between the saints. It also causes the members of the church to grow stronger and more secure in their faith as they pray and fast for one another.

It is clear in the Bible that King Saul, King David, Elijah, Jeremiah, and the apostle Paul all suffered at one time or another as we all do with some mental health disorder such as depression, anxiety, or bipolar disorder. King Saul suffered apparently from depression that was relieved with music played by David; unfortunately, he eventually committed suicide (1 Samuel 16:14–23 KJV). King David cried unto the LORD because his thoughts troubled him, and he feared that his enemy would triumph over him (Psalms 13:2 KJV). Elijah was a prophet and a man of faith, yet he became fearful and fell into depression (1 Kings chapters 18 and 19 KJV). In the book of Jeremiah, Jeremiah is known as the weeping prophet.

He experienced loneliness. He was ridiculed his entire ministry as he preached the Word of God to Judah. The Apostle Paul endured an excessive amount of suffering and affliction for Christ's sake. He asked God seven times to remove an agonizing thorn from his flesh. He was not relieved of it, yet he never gave up on God (2 Corinthians 12:6–7 KJV).

In society today, there are lots of people with mental health illnesses who are functioning well as long as they continue to take their prescribed medication(s) for their condition. Sadly, in the early Christian churches, people with mental health disorders were shunned, imprisoned, and murdered since the authorities of the day were devoid of knowledge about psychiatry and treatment to improve an individual's mental health. It is still difficult to verbalize about one's own personal and family history about mental illness as it affects the core of our well-being. Mental illness is real. Megachurches are seemingly better equipped to assist and refer people with maladjusted behaviors for help since the renowned Pastor Rick Warren openly talked about his son. He announced in 2013 that his twenty-seven-year-old son committed suicide after having a long history of depression; the announcement came through Alyssa Newcomb at ABC news channel. Help and services are available through Christian counselors, psychiatrists, psychologists, and support groups like NAMI (National Alliance of Mental Illness).

According to an article by Brianna Lantz (2019), "Reforming the Church's Response to Mental Illness," she stated that one in five adults every year are diagnosed with some form of mental health disorder that affects their thinking, feeling, and behavior. The church is usually the first place people go when seeking help with their financial, physical, mental, and spiritual problems. The church is thought of as being a place of safety and refuge away from priming eyes, betrayal, and evilness. Since it is reported that 90% of all suicide victims had a mental illness prior to their death, it is incumbent that the church among the leadership and laity have trained experienced people readily available as safety nets for people who are struggling mentally. Information from the CDC stated, "Suicide is the second leading cause of death among people ages 10-24 after accidents" from Anya Kamenetz's, "*The Pandemic Has Researchers worried About Teen Suicide*" (2020).

We, society, or the church cannot look at mental illness as repulsive, disgusting, shocking, demonic, or say that sin is the cause of mental illness. Sin can contribute to feelings of guilt and shame and acting out if the individual does not repent or seek forgiveness because the forces of evil and spiritual weakness are ever present in the church and in our communities. We all must be vigilant, educated, trained, and stay on guard against attacks on the mental health integrity of the members of the church. Warning to all that if the mind gets sick, then soon the body will get sick. Believers ought to be taught that going to the doctor for mental breakdowns is just as important as medical intervention for diabetes, hypertension, and heart disease. God has blessed and given scientists and physicians knowledge and the know how to take care of our bodies and minds. It is in the best interest of believers to follow up on their physical and mental health to prevent and treat illnesses.

Future Portrait of the Christian Church in America in Twenty Years

We are not able to predict what the future holds for the Pentecostal Apostolic churches in the future, only God knows the future. The growth and survival of the church will be in part depended on how we prepare young people to take the helm in growing the church. What we understand is that the way that we used to have church has changed, and it will never be the same as it was. The coronavirus pandemic in 2020 dramatically changed the way that we were used to having church, and it has propelled us to think about having church going forward in new ways. We have had to learn how to use computerized technology to have church using social media platforms. Since we could not meet face-to-face at church without the risk of getting sick and possibly dying from the coronavirus. Therefore, church, as usual, has been restricted. The paradigm for most Christian services since the pandemic was set in motion is through hybrid worship where a percentage of the members physically attend in person and the other attend virtually over the internet. We never seriously thought about merging our live church services with a network before 2020. We have had to rely on electronics devices to reach those churched, unchurched, and those who are not able to attend church. Through the innovation of virtual meeting rooms, some churches have reported an increase in the number of people joining their Sunday morning worship services and Bible classes. A few of them in the chat rooms admitted that they have not set foot inside a church in years so for them social media is the way to worship. The positive aspect of virtual church is that it is helping some people to reconnect to Jesus Christ. Virtual worship online appears to be one of the trends of the future for some church attendees especially for young families and the elderly with medical disabilities.

One pastor, Zach Zehnder (2020), wrote an article titled "10 Bold Predictions About the Future Church in America"; he stated that he and other pastors that he knows had been thinking about the future of the churches in American. He points out that one of the difficult challenges of the pastors in the future will be how to unify their congregation which has been divided. Some people will be attending the physical church, some will be viewing church services online, and some will be undecided. He claimed that it will be difficult for the church to grow and to keep the members engaged in the activities within the church and the surrounding community.

Many people are restless, and their attention span is very short, just about five minutes, he said. The days of having Sunday morning services for three and four hours are in the past. Going forward, members of the church will expect and come prepared for services to be forty-five minutes to one hour. After such times, some will politely excuse themselves and leave the building. For others, services may be reduced to about thirty minutes so that the participants, and viewers online do not become virtually fatigued and disconnect from the social media network. Some may remain logged in but emotionally disconnect themselves during worship when the service is too long in their opinion. Some pastors are considering using virtual action pop-ups on large projection screens like props while preaching their sermons to prevent the audience from being bored. It will be an unimaginable adjustment for traditional worshipper in their late fifty's and beyond to think that church will have to make significant changes to the service format in order to keep churchgoers engaged. Young people today are focused on entertainment, fast interactive screens, and gadgets to keep their attention. So when the Word of God is preached, they become bored if it does not excite them. Preaching does not have to be boring. However, the presentation should be interesting and engaging to the listeners. We do not have the power to save sinners. We can offer timely sermons and pray that as the preached word goes out it will convict the sinner and save the soul.

Many young people do not want to get up early on Sunday morning to attend church. They prefer to get up midmorning and attend church around twelve noon or four o'clock in the afternoon if they go to church at all. While others will get up on Sunday morning and turn on their computers and attend church virtually so that they do not have to get dressed or get their children ready for church. It has been predicted that church attendance will continue to decline over the years. The pandemic introduced us a new way of having church. We learned quickly how to have church virtually online, which we had never thought about before or experienced. We are grateful for the connectivity to social media, but having church online is not the same as being in the house of the Lord with the saints on Sunday mornings in corporate praise, worship, and fellowship.

In Bill Wilson's article, "What will we see less of and more of in America's churches in the 2020s?" he stated that there will be less ministers working full time for the churches because the churches will not be able to pay them a salary. The churches will suffer a lack of funds due to declining family incomes and economic recession. Virtual platforms for Sunday morning worship services will reduce the number of visitors entering through the doors of the church and potential new members. He reported that Christian education institutions are seriously in trouble today, and he expects things to get worse in the coming years due to low enrollment. Wilson commented that face-to-face relationships with new members will be obsolete. New member, current member, and inactive member relationships will probably be initiated, monitored, and maintained by a staff member from the church or a volunteer assigned to oversee those joining the church electronically. Since the coronavirus pandemic, many of us have been reaching out virtually by way of our electronic devices to new church members, current members, those in nursing home and hospitals since we are required to maintain social distancing. Young people and seasoned adults will become less and less interested in human contact, isolate themselves from others and feel content with artificial intelligence and the different social media apps like Instagram, TikTok, Twitter, and others. In the future, church buildings will not be utilized fully for worship and Christian programs. Some may be shared space with other entities or transformed into houses and luxury condos.

Mal Fletcher, a futurist and minister, predicted in his article "Holographic, automation and digital debt: 6 ways the church will look different in 2040" that the church will face many opportunities and challenges over the next forty years. He described how the church will "replace the use of video screen in services" with holographic, 3D dimensional images. The projections on the screens will be lifelike. The use of holographic media will enable pastors, evangelists, and speakers to communicate to larger crowds of people in different parts of the world simultaneously in real time. And it will be interactive by allowing two-way flow of information between the sender and receiver.

Fletcher anticipates that in the future, automation will play a crucial role in our communities and churches from worship services to receipt of offerings and tithes. Thousands of blue-collar workers as well as white-collar workers will be jobless, resulting in a drastic decline in the economy. Paper money is already being replaced with electronic cash apps to receive and send funds and use of debit cards has risen. People will fall into what Fletcher calls "digital debt." Because less cash money will be in their hands, therefore, consumers will be spending more money than what they have due to their dependency on the use of credit cards.

The population status of young people today will be nearing middle age in twenty to forty years. They will be the new leaders of the church in the future so what we pour into them now morally and spiritually is vital to the existence and growth of the Pentecostal Apostolic church. We must devote time and energy to train the youth in the study of God's Word and the appropriate administration of the ministries housed in the churches.

The future church will experience technologies that we have not seen and can only imagine. Scientists and engineers, along with other brilliant professional minds, are working in collaboration with smart, intelligent, adventurous young people to make life on earth fast and simple. They are constantly inventing and putting out new products on the market to seemingly replace human intelligence. We have smartphone, smart television, smart refrigerators, devices, and apps that respond to programmed commands automatically. Wealthy investors and manufacturers are exploring driverless automobiles, and they are planning for automobiles that will someday fly in the air. With so much of the human existence dependent on artificial intelligence, one day in the future, people will not have to leave their homes for anything because everything that a person wants could be delivered to their doorsteps. Basically, anything and everything that a person desires now can be ordered online, and they can get it in a matter of hours or days. Since we are living in a span of time where people, especially young people, want everything quick and effortless for themselves, going to church may become a by-word of the past.

Drones are being used in countless activities for recreation, photography, commercial, private, and the military activities. Drones are utilized to deliver medications to patients in remote regions and hover over traffic jams and accidents on the speedways. In the future, they may transmit images of praise and worship to those who do not want to attend a church setting. In the future, there may not be local neighborhood churches on city street corner as they are now. Small churches could possibly vanish from low, socioeconomic communities. Small congregation may have to gather at each other homes for worship and fellowship if the small churches dissipate. Large megachurches may be used for other venues as more and more young people disassociate themselves from institutionalized religious settings.

A blogger from *Church Leadership Center*, who did not provide his or her identity expressed that in twenty years, the typical local church will, I quote,

- Have 45% of its membership gather for worship on Sunday mornings
- Seek authenticity in worship leaders, but put up with a lot of mediocre music and trite preaching
- Experience continued difficulty finding leaders for congregational oversight and specific ministry initiatives
- Be slowly paying down a 30-year mortgage on a building that no longer seems ministry-friendly
- Feel increasingly isolated from its immediate neighborhood and the current culture
- Find its membership numbers plateaued or declining.

We do not know what the Christian church will look like in twenty years. As far as its locality, program functionality, or population configuration, what is vital to the existence and growth of the Pentecostal Apostolic church is the manifestation of the spirit of God in it and the preaching of the gospel of Jesus Christ according to scripture. Satan will continue to defy the work of Christ. But we have this hope from Jesus Christ Himself: "Upon this rock I will build my church; and the gates of hell shall not prevail against it" (Matthew 16:18 KJV). There may be many small churches operating separately but combined on the day of the Lord's return, they will make up the one church, the body of Christ. The church that Jesus build will not fail; it will last forever.

Chapter 3

Roles of Family Dynamics

According to authors Bahareh Jabbari and Audra S. Rouster, *family dynamics* refers to the "pattern of interactions among relatives, their roles and relationships, and the various factors that shape their interactions." Family interactions with each other whether positive or negative play a major role in the development of a child. Children are great imitators of what they see adults do, especially their parents. What the child or children observe and experience in their daily lives forms their character and personality as demonstrated through child's play, engagement with playmates, peers, and family members. Children copy their parents and significant adult figures in their lives, then at some point in their lives, they decide who they want to be like growing into adulthood. Bonding relationships within the family can offer feelings of security or stress.

Traditionally, financial, ethnical, intellectual, political, and belief patterns held by families are passed down from one generation to the other. But sometimes, they are altered when the next generation discovers a different way of doing things.

Years ago, the family unit was the fundamental core in most societies in America. Families chose to live together in multi-family structures with their grandparents, parents, children, and sometimes with one or two extended family members. There was no confusion about the roles of men, women, or children in the homes. Fathers taught their sons to work and defend the family. Mothers taught their daughters to cook, keep house, nurture, and care for the young ones. Parents went out to work, children went to school, and the grandparents took care of the small children that did not attend school. Families had a sense of obligation to take into their home anyone from the immediate or extended family who was sick. And they took care of them until they got better, or they did not need care anymore. Families collaboratively celebrated the joys of a new home, a new baby, graduation, communion, and joining a church together. Families were supportive to each other during times of sorrows as well. Each person in the family unit was loved, nurtured, protected, and reprimanded as needed by the eldest in the household and sometimes by neighbors on the street where they lived.

Families some twenty to thirty years ago were warm, inviting, compassionate, and intuitive. Members of the family and community attended their church weekly to monthly; church was important in keeping the family together. The church was the place to go to if one needed assistance with food, utility bills, housing, and other socioeconomic matters for the family. Spiritual development was exercised by families reading Bible stories together and children learning Bible verses from the book of Psalm. Most people knew or at least heard about the golden rule, and they respected it: "Do unto others as you would have them do unto you" (Matthew 7:12 KJV). Parents used to spend time training and educating their children about life's rewards and consequences. Families learned about God in the church, and the teachings were followed up at home. There was a time when parents took their children to church, but as time passed, parents started sending their children to church instead of going to church with them. Today, it is difficult to get children and adults to come to church because they are not interested. They have filled up their calendars with busy activities deliberately to keep themselves out of church. Therefore, the family is falling further and further from knowledge and engagement with the Lord Jesus Christ. Conversations with our modern-day youth revealed that many of their friends their age have never in their life been inside of a church for a service not even for a funeral. Shockingly, this generation of millennials, along with generation Z, are growing up without any religious identity or affiliation mainly due to the lack of Christian identity and affiliation of their parents. Our parents, a few decades ago, held us children accountable for what they had taught us. They made us go to church every Sunday whether we felt like it or not. They were tenacious about keeping Sundays free of activities so that we could attend church, they drilled in us that "It is the Lord's Day." We were expected and accountable to be in church on Sunday unless we had to work.

Parents Living Double Lives

In *Collins Cobuild Dictionary*, *double life* is defined as, "If you say that someone is living a double life, you mean that they lead two separate and very different lives, and they appear to be a different person in each."

Parents are their children's first teachers, and children more than likely will do and say what they see and hear their parents do. Children are usually inspired by their parents. They want to be like their parents naturally and spiritually when they become adults. We have observed children of politicians, professionals, famous people, and spiritual leaders who are following in their parents' footsteps. They strive to carry on a legacy in the memory of their parents and family name.

Parents have the power to influence their children to live for Jesus Christ or to reject him. For years, it was thought and believed that the way Christians were seen in church was the way that they acted when they were at home; unfortunately, that was not always true in the homes. Some parents were living a double life. An individual living a double life is a hypocrite, a pretender. Generally, if someone is living a double life, it is not evident until the person is caught in a lie or something terrible happens that exposes the person as a hypocrite. Recorded in the gospels repeatedly are the words of Jesus who condemned and rebuked the Scribes and Pharisees for being hypocrites (Matthew 23:1–39 and Luke 11:37–54). Hypocrisy is a sin. McGibbon's article (2018), "The Psychology of a Double Life," pointed out that a hypocrite should understand that living a double life is inevitably destructive due to the person constantly attempting to conceal their dark secrets. Eventually, those dark secrets will negatively affect their relationships with their family, friends, employer, and co-laborers in Christ.

Children are very sensitive to mood swings in their family members. They can intuitively sense when something is wrong, or when someone is not acting like themselves. Parents who are living a double life will find it difficult to spend time with their children, family, and spend time in prayer and fellowship at church. They will come up with all sorts of excuses why they do not have time. Long periods of absences, erratic behavior, and broken promises by parents are warning signs that something has gone awry. We cannot be good parents or a good servant of Jesus Christ if we are living a double life. The scripture in James 1:6–8 (KJV) let us know that "a double minded man is unstable in all his ways." The double-minded person's life will start to spiral downward further and further as the situation gets worse and worse. Christians cannot serve two masters at the same time nor can they walk with Christ if they have one foot in the church and the other foot in the world. Every one, young and old, must make a choice either to serve the Lord or the devil.

Parenting is not a stroll in the park; it is hard work. Every parent has a mandate from God to "train up a child in the way that he should go and when he is old, he will not depart from it" (Proverbs 22:6 KJV). Also, the scripture instructs us not to stand in the way of sinners or sit in the seat of scorners (Psalm 1:1 KJV). If we are not living a godly life before our children, then we are an obstruction and hindrance to them. Moreover, inconsistent wavering behaviors and ungodly attitudes from parents can send mixed messages to their children, which leads to a pattern and practice of hypocrisy like their parents. Living a double life over time destroys the faith of the current family, and it has the tendency to disintegrate any seeds of faith that was planted in the next generation. Some young people are exploring strange religious philosophies and theories contrary to the Bible because they observed in the home that their parents were not committed adherents to the doctrine of Jesus Christ. Parents who live double lives are not true disciples of Christ. Christian parents have a moral and spiritual obligation to be an example before their children. They should live appropriately and righteously to have their children mimic them. The scripture requires that we mark the perfect man and behold the upright knowing that the sinner will be destroyed (Psalms 37:37 KJV). It is the job of parents to imprint their children with the necessary skills that will prepare them for serving in the kingdom of God and living a lifestyle of holiness.

Pastor Todd Phillips (2016) wrote a blog and appeared on a YouTube video titled "How NOT to Lead a Double Life." His article was very interesting and presented some helpful tips to avoid the traps of sin and Satan. He advised the believers to read the Bible daily and keep their minds and thoughts on the contents of the scriptures that they have read. Also, a note of importance is to have a close friend to confide in or someone who is genuinely concerned about one's welfare and spiritual maturity. Everyone needs a friend or mentor who will honestly point out their weaknesses so that they do not succumb to pitfalls of temptation. All Christians should be alert and aware of the devices of Satan. We should avoid the allurement to try some new things offered by the tempter. It is impossible to walk so close to the edge of a cliff without one day falling off. Sin is contagious, and we cannot be yoked up with sin and think that it will not contaminate us because it will. Jesus told us to fight against, stand firm against the devil and do not give in to him and after a while, the devil will run away from us (James 4:7 KJV). We must resist the temptations of the flesh at all costs with the help of the Holy Ghost through Jesus Christ.

Blended Families with Different Religious Beliefs

A blended family may be called a stepfamily or just simply a family. Literally, "a blended family is defined as a family made of two parents and their children from previous marriages" (yourdictionary.com). The scriptures provide us with accounts of blended families in the Bible from the patriarchs Abraham, Jacob, King David to our Lord Jesus Christ; these were all members of blended families. In ancient cultures, members of blended families adopted or assimilated into the religious beliefs of the head of the household, usually the father. It is the responsibility of both parents, father, and mother, to teach their children the Bible and faith in Jesus Christ. From the words of Apostle Paul, he encourages children to honor and obey their parents in all things that are right (Colossians 3:20 KJV). Furthermore, parents are to teach their children about God at home and throughout the day as they are completing their daily activities of living as found in Deuteronomy 6:6–7 (KJV). Initially, God intended parents to teach, instruct, and guide their own children at home rather than sending them out of the home to paid teachers, tutors, and institutions. Christian families need to teach and embrace the gospel message and impress upon their children that Jesus Christ died for their sins. Jesus is Lord and king. They can trust in him to help them in times of trouble. Each generation needs to be taught that Jesus Christ is coming back one day to take the righteous to heaven to live with him.

Marriages between young people of different faiths or religious beliefs occur about 39% in America. Research has shown that young adults reported that having a spouse of the same religion was not important to them. "Interfaith marriage is common in U.S, particularly among the recently wed" according to Caryle Murphy's (2015) article. Men and women are not staying married to each other long. They are not working on keeping their marriages intact. We acknowledge there is no guarantee that marriage will work between a couple or that they will stay together until one of them die. However, Christian couples need to understand that marriage is an institution ordained by God and they must work together to maintain their marriages. When couples stand to take their vows, they are doing so in the presence of God and the witnesses who came to attend their wedding. The scripture says it is better not to make a vow than to make a vow and break it (Ecclesiastes 5:4–6). Couples must remember that God is a witness to them taking their marriage vows, and he heard them confess their unfailing love to each other. In scriptures, God's holy word is quite adamant how a man is to love his wife and how the wife is to honor her husband (Genesis 2:24; Proverbs

18:22; Mark 10:8–12; Ephesians 5:25–33; 1 Corinthians 7:39; 1 Peter 3:1–5, KJV).

A study conducted in 2015 by the Pew Research Group, showed that "39 percent of Americans who'd married since 2010 had a spouse of a different religion," according to article writer Alison Bowen at the Chicago Tribune, "Interfaith marriage is common in U.S." Marriage of people of the same faith, let alone an interfaith marriage can be challenging if they are not willing to respect, submit, and love each other unconditionally. Moreover, a believer who goes and marry an unbeliever, one who is not baptized in Jesus's name or who does not believe in the Lord Jesus Christ as their savior, shows an outward display of disobedience to the scripture. Apostle Paul warned the believers at Corinth, "Be ye not unequally yoked together with unbelievers: for what fellowship hath righteousness with unrighteousness? And what communion hath light with darkness?" (2 Corinthians 6:14 KJV).

Most religions expect and some require that couples be of the same faith before marriage. Catholics require non-Catholics to convert, and Muslims require non-Muslims to convert to their religion prior to marriage; otherwise the priest or imam will not perform the marriage ceremony. The question that comes to mind is why are apostolic born-again believers marrying unsaved persons? When the Bible clearly admonishes us not to do it. Quite a few in this younger generation think that they can disregard God's word without consequences, so they are ignoring the teaching and marrying unsaved people. Some have declared that they will get him or her saved after they get married. Historically, if an individual has not been converted before marriage, it is very unlikely to happen after marriage except the Lord changes the heart of the unbeliever. The reason being, since he or she has gotten the person that they wanted to marry, the unbelieving spouse does not feel obligated to change their religion or nonreligious affiliation.

To further complicate matters in blended families is the issue of what faith will the child or children be raised in. We are witnesses of the decline in teenagers and young people attendance at church on Sundays. Blended families who have not resolved the issue of how to raise their children together in the Pentecostal Apostolic church prior to marriages are less likely to agree on having all the family at the one church. Unbelieving spouses in blended families "are not likely to go through the effort of making it to Sunday services or raising their families in the faith," clearly stated in Stonestreet and Morris (2020) article, "Why Young People Leave the Church and Why They Stay."

We have observed grievously that the convictions of the unbelieving spouse are stronger than the believing spouse when it comes down to which church, they are going to raise their children in. As a result, the family ends up either going to a nondenominational church or they stop going to church all together. One of the consequences of marrying an unbeliever is that the children in the family are not brought up in the Apostolic faith. Because the weak believing parent yields to the unbelieving parent and the believing parents loses the battle over doctrinal education. Secondly, the teenagers and young adults in that family are added to the growing list of young people who are no longer attending church or leaving the Pentecostal Apostolic faith. When children are not raised Apostolic in blended families and taught consistently about Jesus Christ, they are subject to fall away from going to church when they become adults.

To decrease the number of teenagers and young adults from leaving the faith, it is strongly advised that potential couples seek God for his approval and adhere to godly wise counsellors on who they should marry. Also, after marriage, and starting a family, it is utmost important for couples to prioritize teaching and raising their children in the tradition of the Apostolic faith so that their children and grandchildren will continue in it with the help of the Lord.

Preacher's Kid Syndrome

According to Wikipedia, "Preacher's kid is a term to refer to a child of a preacher, pastor, deacon, vicar, lay leader, priest, minister, or other similar church leader. Although the phrase can be used in a purely descriptive way, it may also be used as a stereotype. There are two different stereotypes of the preacher's kid: in one, they are perfectly angelic role models, in the other they are rebels at the opposite extreme. The existence of these stereotypes is a source of pressure on children of clergy."

A pastor along with his or her family are in the limelight and scrutinized twenty-four hours a day, seven days a week by people inside and outside of the church, looking at them. They are adored, watched, followed, and mimicked on account of their physical attractiveness, intelligence, popularity, perceived wealth, and sense of spirituality. As noted by Vanderbloemen (2018) article, "11 Things a Pastor's Kid May Be Thinking—That You May Not Even Realize," some people in the church celebrate the pastor and the pastor's family while others are just waiting for them to fall from grace. There is a lot of pressure on the pastor's children to live up to the expectation of the churched and unchurch. They are expected to be perfect by some people. The children are reminded to live their lives as pleasing unto God and do not make their parents' shame.

Being a pastor or spouse of a pastor is not an easy job; this researcher knows firsthand. It requires the man or woman of God to spend an extraordinary amount of time away from their family to work in the development of church ministries and maintain them. Pastors really do not have days off per se; it is a demanding occupation. Because of the demand on the pastor, unconsciously, he or she may transfer that same demand onto their children, leaving them to spend long hours without their parents or spend long hours at the church while everyone else has gone home. The pastor's kids, on multiple occasions and levels, are drafted into aspects of the ministry when no one comes forward or volunteer to do the task at hand. Often, pastors, preachers, missionaries, deacons, and other religious leaders thoughtlessly put their children into positions of leadership that they do not desire and sometimes are not qualified to do. On occasions, it works out but other times it does not workout favorably for the preacher's kids or congregation.

When the children, teenagers, and young adults are thrust into unfamiliar and uncomfortable settings it can be traumatic for them. To avoid creating emotions of frustration, angry, bitterness, outrage, and dislike toward the church. Everyone should remember that these young people are human beings just like they are. They should be treated with the same respect and consideration as any other young person at the church. During research for this project some young people have voiced that they have felt disrespected, used, overwhelmed, and unappreciated in view of the fact that their parents are always relying on them to function in the church ministries.

Pastors who are parents should realize that their children need them as parents first then pastors. The guidelines in the Bible admonished, "But if any provide not for his own, and specially for those of his own house, he hath denied the faith, and is worse than an infidel" (1 Timothy 5:8 KJV). A spiritual leader's responsibility is to their family first then to the church that they serve; otherwise, they run the risk of losing their spouse and their children. Young and adult children need unconditional love, genuine care, and quality time with their parents. Family togetherness and connectiveness are essential in keeping the family unit intact. The parent-pastor relationship with their children can be the deciding factor between their young and adult children staying in the church or leaving the church. Some young adults leave the church simply because they are suffering from burnout and lack of attention and affection from their parent-pastor. We have heard sorrowfully, pastors confess from the pulpit that they gained many converts to the church but lost their children to things in the world because they did not designate time with their own children.

The Bible provides us with clear examples of parents who did not spend adequate or quality time at home with their children. Though their children had access to the temple and participated in the temple service, their hearts were not committed to doing what was just and righteous. The prophet Eli was near in vicinity to his sons, but he did not correct them or stand up to Hophni and Phinehas. He did not stop them from stealing the Lord's portion of the sacrifices or sleeping with the women. They willingly committed moral and spiritual sin without remorse. They were killed in battle with the Philistines at Aphek (1 Samuel 1–4 KJV); apparently, sin hasted their deaths.

The prophet Samuel, on the other hand, was absence a lot from his sons while traveling to deliver messages to the people from the Lord. The consequence of an absence father is lawless sons. When

Samuel became an old man, his sons turned away from serving God and as judges in Israel they took bribes and corrupted the justice system for the people (1 Samuel 8:1–1 KJV). The scripture describes the prophet Samuel as a good man who served Jehovah God from his childhood. Nonetheless, his sons did not continue their walk in their father's footsteps; they publicly embarrassed him. This illustration showed that children raised in a devout home with a righteous servant-father does not preclude the temptations of Satan. As noted with the upbringing of Eli and Samuel's sons, children brought up by priestly parents does not guarantee that the children will do everything right. Parents must correct their children when they are wrong or run the risk of losing them to sin and death. We cannot save our children from sin, but we can pray for them that God will give them a broke and contrite heart of repentance. Only God can save them.

The call to pastor is a call from God to the pastor not to the pastor's kids. Though having the entire family on board to support the pastor's call to ministry is a blessing, it is still challenging to the preacher's kids. Depending on the size of the religious organization and size of the church, the pastor may have to relocate as directed by the board of directors to a new church for a pastoral assignment. This can be troublesome and stressful for the children, especially adjusting to a new home, new school, loss of old friends and making new ones.

As mentioned earlier, being a preacher's kid is challenging. Ryan A. French (2021) points out in his article "4 Problems Preacher's Kids Face" some interesting details that the preacher's kids may experience. Some preacher's kids suffer in silence because they do not want to cause pain and discomforts to their parents or leaders; therefore, they keep quiet and isolate themselves. Generally, the preacher's kid feels like they do not have trusting peers or a confidant that they can openly talk to without their conversation getting back to the pastor. They are lonely.

Preacher's kids see the best and worst of the people that their parents serve. When their parents are ridiculed, falsely accused, blamed for some oversight or misfortune or there is an attempt to assassinate their character, the preacher's kid is indirectly involved. They feel and see the unhappiness and misery of their parents. They see the ugly side of Christianity and Christians. Some congregations have had physical fist fights in the church because church people verbally attacked the preacher's kids. The preacher's kids are not special or different from other kids however, they do have to share their parents with so many people. That's why it is vitally important for pastors to set aside blocked time to be alone with their family. And make every effort to support their children at their school events and special programs. Children, teenagers, young adults need to see and feel the love of their parents-pastors because when the church lose the preacher's kids, the church also loses its future leaders.

Social Struggles of Teenagers and Young Adults

This generation of teenagers and young adults are dealing with social issues that previous generations never dealt with. We have heard from older people that said they are so glad that they were born when they were born because they do not think that they would survive this era. Many parents, grandparents, and mature adults in the church have expressed grave concerns over the lack of morality and insolent behavior of young people born to millennials and generations Z. What is going to happen to them in the future socially and spiritually after their parents, grandparents, and significant adult figures are gone? The apostle Paul spoke to Timothy and warned him that radical changes would occur in the church after his demise. He told his son in the gospel that some would have a form of godliness and misrepresent the faith and hypocrisy would be on the up rise. False teachers would teach perverse doctrines which would pull people away from Christ (2 Timothy 3:1–5 KJV). We are already hearing and seeing the deterioration of religious, ethical, and moral standards that used to be commonly upheld by saints and sinners.

Multiple young people today do not have filters over their mouths. They are bold when they speak about things that they do not like or accept. They say whatever they want to say to whomever they want to say it. And they do whatever come to their minds without hesitation or thought about the consequences. Many have been reportedly disrespectful toward their elderly family members at home and at church. For many of them not in the church and for some that are in the church, their profiles can be described as narcissistic, selfish, thoughtless, impatient, uncooperative, aggressive, and greedy for money. They do not want to do anything for free. Several of them want to be paid for assisting family members at home. They want to be paid for their service in any capacity at the house of the Lord or they will not do it. They openly resist and defy corrective criticisms from those in authority such parents, teachers, politicians, and pastors. Over the years, there has been a deterioration of etiquette and respect from young people due to their parents and guardian's toleration of their disrespectful and ill manners. Such bad behaviors have spilled over out of the homes into society as normal behavior and slowly they have inched their way into the church environment. This generation of youths are extremely weak minded and temperamental about almost everything. They need much prayer and spiritual interventions by caring but firm instructors and counselors to redirect them in the paths of righteousness so they can change their despicable ways.

As mentioned previously, this generation of teenagers and young adults are faced with many social issues, and they are stressed as never before about almost everything. They are suffering from depression, anxiety, isolation, sexual disorientation (homosexuality), homelessness, and suicide to list a few detailed from Bruce's (2020) article "Teen Depression." Parents, guardians, and adult significant others need to be aware of their teens' behavior and seek medical treatment if their teen's moods or sadness does not improve in a couple of weeks. Some teens and young adults will not mature to complete adulthood or reach their full potential in life without the professional help, love, and attention from caring people and the grace of God. Young people have needs in society and in the church. However, some of them are looking to fill the emptiness inside of them in the wrong places. We cannot deny their problems or look away expecting them to disappear. They are not going away on their own. We must embrace this generation of youths and encourage them to call on the name of Jesus Christ for help and deliverance. Jesus Christ is able to fix and take them through their problems.

About thirteen years ago, smartphones became a part of our lives along with social media networks. Now most of us cannot live without our cell phones, they are with us nearly everywhere we go. We are bombarded constantly with information solicited and unsolicited from numerous notifications on our cell phones and email addresses. Electronic information is causing mental fatigue and social overload in people of all ages.

Numerous young people are influenced negatively by comments and pictures that they see on Facebook, Instagram, Twitter, TikTok, and other internet platforms. These easy, quick, and accessible medias are contributing to how our young people view and value themselves and others. While smartphones and social media platforms can be beneficial, they can also be harmful and dangerous in some cases.

Social worker Amy Morin (2020) in her article points out "Top 10 Social Issues Teens Struggle with Today. Technology Has Changed or Amplified the Struggles Young People Face." She stated that an estimated 3.2 million adolescents reported that they had suffered from depression in 2017 that is according to The National Institute of Mental Health. Some 20% of teens reported having been bullied as documented by the National Center for Education Statistic. Bullying in any form is a bad thing. However, cyberbullying is the most common method that young people are using to attack other young people. Teenagers are being singled out because they are different from regular kids. Bullies are aggressive toward some young people because they do not like them, or they see them as easy targets to pick on. Peer pressure is a huge problem for teens over social media. Teens are being coerced into showing inappropriate photographs (sexting) of themselves over the internet. They think that it will stop the bullying, or it will be a course of action of acceptance, unknowingly to the naive teens, it can have serious consequences on them later in life.

Other teens and young adults are drinking alcohol to cope with stress in their lives, which can lead to dependency on other intoxicating substances and drugs. Texting on social media is so prevalent today until many teens and young people are inept to verbally communicate. Verbal communication among the youth seemingly is a dying skill. They do not know how to talk to each other. They text in fragmented sentences and use emojis like crazy instead of commenting on how they are feeling. Teens and young people appear to need to be reminded and retrained on how to sit down across from each other and look the person in the eyes and talk, hold an intelligent conversation without their cell phones. Whether young people understand it or not communication is paramount. It is necessary to engage in conversation with people to build healthy relationships inside and outside the church.

Another issue among youths briefly discussed was their pursuit of a college education. Several of the teenagers and young adults brought up in the church have entered college unprepared for living on the college campus. College campuses come with many demands and challenges for the unsuspected Christian youth especially, those attending non-Christian colleges. Teenagers and young adults may be invited to partake in activities that are happening on campus grounds or in clubs that exposes them to alcohol use, drug doping, promiscuity, and other ungodly acts. For those Christians who have never been away from home, these types of activities can influence them to try some of these things because they are new and different to them. It is necessary and important for young people to remember that they are to put on the whole armor of God. Wear it at all times so that they will be protected and able to stand against Satan and his tools of destruction (Ephesians 6:11 KJV). Overtime, some who are not anchored in the Word of God or are weak in their faith will fall to temptations.

Unknowingly, parents and church leaders have not appropriately educated the youth well enough on how to recognize and avoid the traps, tricks, and enticements of sin on college grounds. Harrison (2018) wrote "Christian College Students Face Challenges at Public Universities" where they are meeting oppositions and objections in the classrooms to their theological beliefs and Christian lifestyle on non-Christian colleges. They are forced sit in classrooms and auditoriums with other young people who do not have a relationship with the Lord. They cannot opt out of these classrooms. Students are being academically taught their course work by teachers and professors who are nonbelievers. Reportedly, many of the teachers and professors are atheists and proponents of strange philosophies that they are forcing upon Christian students. Some of these educators have been known to intimidate teenagers and young adult students intentionally in an effort to persuade them to join cults, Catholicism and Islamic groups based on the campuses. As unacceptable as this may be innumerable teenagers and young adults are pressured by their peers and other influences to be a part of the in-crowd. The reality is that if the Christian students are not rooted and ground in their beliefs, they most likely will succumb to secularism in order to fit in.

Behind closed doors at college, several young Christians who were interviewed by this researcher stated that they tried to conceal what was stressing them out and they tried to cope with their issues alone. Misguided and afraid, they confessed to suffering in silence. They also did not talk about the problems since they were ashamed. Though most young people want to be independent of their parents and adult authoritative figures in their life, they usually will welcome a listening ear, a shoulder to lean on, and expressions of kindness and love from caring adults. To better equip the youths, we can encourage them to talk freely about their problems without judgment and assist them with their needs they best way that we can without making them feel shame, dirty, and unforgiven.

Young people are struggling, and they need a sense of hope from adults. We can spend more quality time with them in one-on-one meetings and small group conference settings to discuss things that are on their minds. It is a good way to let the young people know that we care about them, and we are available to listen to them. We can share our stories with the young people and let them know that we all have struggles in this world. We have all made mistakes that we wish we could change. Life is difficult at time for everyone. Offer messages of hope that Jesus will help them. Encourage them to read their Bible daily and meditate on the goodness of the Lord. Guide them on how to ask the Lord to help them in making good decisions instead of being impulsive. Let them know that we are praying for them and their success in college and life.

To better prepare young Christians for their college experiences, the church leaders and youth leaders could host pre-college events with workshops, professional speakers, and postgraduates to educate the perspective college students on the aspects of college life and how to avoid the pitfalls. This will allow attendees to make inquiries and act out scenarios that encompasses campus life. The goal of such platforms would be to achieve the highest possible retention rate of teenagers and young adult churchgoers who are going off to college and returning to the church after completion of their education. Youths who are preeducated and pretrained on how to live away from home will be able to stand against the depravity and moral decay seen on college campuses.

Chapter 4

Methodology

Data information for this study on the exploration of the decline and impact of young people not attending church after high school and college was obtained from a simple survey questionnaire written by this researcher. The survey was created through the Survey Monkey App; the link to it was SurveyMonkey.com. This undertaking solicited the assistance of pastors and Christian youth leaders affiliated with the Pentecostal Apostolic fellowship of churches. The pastors and youth leaders were from small churches with congregations less than one hundred members. The geographics comprised of areas along the northeast corridor from New York, New Jersey, Pennsylvania, Maryland, down to North Carolina and South Carolina.

Pastors and youth leaders were contacted on their cell phones and through their email addresses by this researcher. The purpose of the study was explained to them, and the timeframe allotted for the completion of the survey questionnaire was discussed. They were informed that the survey consisted of a total of twenty questions, and it would take about ten minutes to complete. The answers were multiple choice, and the potential candidates would type their answers onto the survey in the blanket spaces provided. The survey was available on the Survey Monkey App in two pages. Because of the Survey Monkey format, only ten questions could be entered on a page at a time; therefore, the survey was divided into part 1 and part 2 due to the automated design. The survey was opened for responses from the candidates on Survey Monkey for seven weeks from February 8, 2021, through March 20, 2021, then it was closed. The Survey Monkey application download and use was free to all candidates who responded.

A letter addressed to the pastors and youth leaders was emailed to them as affirmation in the pursuit of this research study. As delineated in the letter, the project criteria focused on teenagers and young adults ages from eighteen (18) to twenty-nine (29) years old who had graduated from high school, entered college, or graduated from college. More specifically, individuals in this age range whose attendance have fallen off or have stopped coming to church on Sunday and midweek Bible study.

A copy of the survey questionnaire and letter that was addressed to the teenagers and young adults was sent to the pastors and youth leaders by emailed so that they could keep a copy for their records. An introductory letter that explained the research study was sent to all the potential candidates who were referred to the researcher. The candidates were informed that their participation with the survey was voluntary, and their identity would be kept anonymous. There were no identification markers on the survey so that the participants could freely and honestly answer the questions without fear of their identity being found out or any type of reprisal to them.

Immediately, the pastors and youth leaders were interested, and they showed enthusiasm in our discussion of the problem at hand in the church. Many of the pastors and youth leaders acknowledged that they were losing young people from their churches, and they were not returning. These clerics and youth leaders communicated that they noticed the problem, but they had not thought about any proactive methods or strategies to interrupt the decline of young churchgoers. The researcher proposed to arrange a group meeting on Zoom with the pastors and youth leaders who referred names of candidates for the study in the hope that the findings from the research study will reduce and prayerfully prevent teenagers and young adults from leaving the church. Due to the serious nature of this phenomena and its unforeseen impact globally on Christian churches, it needs to be addressed and discussed with spiritual leaders and parents in Pentecostal Apostolic churches.

As discussed with the pastors and youth leaders, the names and email addresses of potential candidates to complete the survey were sent to the researcher's mobile phone and email address as requested. After the names and email addresses of the teenagers and young people were received an introductory letter with details of the survey was emailed to them by the researcher. The researcher did not store the respondents' names or email addresses since it was a condition of the survey agreement to remain anonymous. Approximately 107 candidates were contacted by emailed with a copy of the introductory letter and link to Survey Monkey to complete the survey questionnaire. Only three introductory letters, along with the survey questionnaires, were mailed using the United States Postal Service as requested. They were mailed with a self-addressed stamped returned envelope to the researcher. The total number of introductory letters and survey questionnaires distributed was 110.

Among the twenty-three pastors and youth leaders contacted, only twelve of them submitted names, emails addresses, and physical addresses of persons that they thought would participate in the research study. The contact information of the teenagers and young adults was texted to the researcher's cellular phone or email address by the participating pastors and youth leaders.

Limitations of Surveys and Analyses

The survey questionnaire was limited to responses from teenagers and young adults aged eighteen to twenty-nine years old who are not attending or have left the Christian churches after finishing high school, entered, or graduated from college. Only Pentecostal Apostolic churches located demographically on the east coast were targeted and engaged in this study. More specifically, those Pentecostal Apostolic churches within the fellowship of churches along the northeast corridor from New York, New Jersey, Pennsylvania, Maryland, down to North Carolina and South Carolina. Teenagers and young adults were referred to this researcher for participation in the survey from male and female clerics and youth leaders in different organizations and dioceses. The size of their assemblies was considered small because the congregations were less than one hundred members. There were 110 survey questionnaires in total sent out via email and postal mail. The would-be participants had the option to complete the survey online through the Survey Monkey link or by having a copy of the survey mailed to them with an enclosed return self-addressed stamped envelope to the researcher. The identity of the respondents was kept anonymous. There were no characteristic markers attached or connected to the survey to recognize the persons who filled it out.

Three surveys were mailed using the United States Postal Services to the potential respondents as requested. But they were never returned to the researcher in the self-addressed return envelopes.

According to Survey Monkey insight analysis of Part 1 of the survey, there was a total of forty-four responses to part 1 of the survey. The completion rate was 100%. The typical time spent on the survey was one minute and forty-seven seconds. The most skipped question was Question 10: "Please select the reason you do not regularly attend church." It was skipped by three of the forty-four respondents.

According to the Survey Monkey insight analysis of part 2 of the survey, there was a total of thirty-five responses. Completion rate was 100%. The typical time spent answering the survey questions was five minutes and twenty-three seconds. The most skipped question here was Question 10: "Do you have any comments or suggestions for the church leaders?" This question was skipped by four of the thirty-five respondents.

Survey Responses

The following are the survey questions from part 1 and the percentages of the responses:

1. Were you born and raised in the apostolic church that you attended?
    70.00% responded "Yes"
    30.00% responded "No"

2. Which did you attend?
   70.00% responded "Sunday school"
   22.50% responded "Bible class"
   7.50% responded "None"
3. Did the church have new member classes for new members?
   35.00% responded "Yes"
   65.00% responded "No"
4. How would you describe the members of the church?
   45.00% responded "Friendly"
   37.50% responded "Compassionate"
   2.50% responded "Mean-spirited"
   0.00% responded "Rude"
   15.00% responded "Cliquish/nonwelcoming"
   0.00% responded "Cold and uninviting"
5. How would you rate your relationship with the pastor(s) & church leadership?
   2.50% responded "Poor"
   27.50% responded "Fair"
   25.00% responded "Good"
   45.00% responded "Excellent"
6. What need did the church help you with?
   7.50% responded "Transportation"
   2.50% responded "Health issues"
   0.00% responded "Financial hardship"
   70.00% responded "Spiritual"
   20.00% responded "Other"
7. Was the teaching and preaching of the Bible clear to you?
   92.50% responded "Yes"
   7.50% responded "No"
8. Did you participate on any of the following?
   65.00% responded "Praise Team/Choir/Music Ministry"
   15.00% responded "Youth/Young Adult Ministry"
   7.50% responded "Usher/Hospitality"
   5.00% responded "Other"
   7.50% responded "None"

9. Would you say that you felt safe at the church?
   90.00% responded "Yes"
   10.00% responded "No"
10. Please select the reason you do not regularly attend church.
   18.92% responded "Was offended by someone at the church"
   21.62% responded "Had a difficult time fitting in with other young people"
   10.81% responded "Church was boring"
   48.65% responded "Have to work on the weekends"

Summary of the responses to the survey questions in Part 1 was a little surprising to the researcher. Nearly half of the teenagers and young adults (48.65%) notably responded that they were absent from church because they were working on the weekends.

With so many youths working on Sundays, it is unimaginable that they had not thought of requesting to be off on Sundays for religious purposes. Most jobs are accommodating and will let people off on Sundays for religious reasons if the employees ask or agree to work every Saturday. Working every Saturday would allow the workers, youth in this case, to attend church on Sundays.

According to the findings, 70% of the teenagers and young adults surveyed said that they were born and raised in the Apostolic church, and they went to Sunday school. We can only hope and pray that the word that they heard early in their lives will stir them up to come back to the Lord's house as they are getting older and taking on adult responsibilities.

Though 92.50% of the teenagers and young people indicated that the teaching and preaching of the Word was clear to them somehow it is difficult to accept that they understood it since they left the church. A study conducted a few years ago by the American Enterprise Institute reported that once upon a time when millennials left the church they came back when they became adults and had a family, but now it appears that when they leave the church they are not returning.

The question that came to mind was did they really understand the word when they attended the church? Did they apply the word to themselves that they heard and read? The Bible reminds us in James 1:22–25 to not be a hearer but a doer of the Word:

> But be ye doer of the word, and not hearers only, deceiving your own selves. For if any be a hearer of the word, and not a doer, he is like unto a man beholding his natural face in a glass: For he beholdeth himself, and goeth his way, and straightway forgetteth what manner of man he was...he being not a forgetful hearer, but a doer of the work, this man shall be blessed in his deed.

Hearing and reading the word without combining it with faith is inoperative; it is not working.

Tragically, many have fallen prey to sin because the word was not truly in their hearts and minds. They did not remember the Word.

Not surprising that participation in the musical department was at 65% response rate. A high number showed that teenagers and young adults were attracted to music. And it kept many of them actively engaged in the church for a period of time. Most young people enjoy singing or playing a musical instrument. They use much of their energy in motion. It has been shown that physical activity as oppose to a sedentary lifestyle generates dopamine and serotonin, which makes people happy. Young people were apparently happy when they were active. Oddly enough, 65% of the respondents indicated that their particular congregation did not have new member classes. May be a prerequisite to joining the musical department could be the completion of a new member class so that each member would understand their role and responsibility in the stability and growth of their church.

Noted in the survey responses that 45% of the teenagers and young adults indicated that the congregation that they were apart of was friendly; 37.50% were compassionate and 15% thought that their assemble was cliquish or nonwelcoming to outsiders. The survey equally showed 45% of the respondents had an excellent relationship with their pastor or church leadership. Another group, 25% identified their relationship as good and 27% as fair. On a whole, just looking at the numbers, these congregations and participants seemingly were satisfactory with each other's contact for a while.

The church apparently met the spiritual needs of the teenagers and young adults at 70% of the time. They indicated that they had other nonspecified needs that the church assisted them with 20% of the time; what were those needs we cannot tell. Perhaps the participants personally or privately explained their situation to the church leadership for help. Transportation apparently was not an issue at 7.50% that prevented them from attending church or health issues at 2.50%. Young people are active and strong; they can walk longer and faster than adults and generally are in better health than adults which may account for low transportation and health issues percentage on the survey.

The following are the survey questions for part 2 and the participants' responses:

Survey questions below for part 2 and the data trends did not apply to this section because the answers to these questions were sentences or short narratives from the respondents.

1. What was the most difficult thing for you being in an apostolic church?
2. While at college were you able to find a church and go to it?
3. Were you able to meet with other Christians on campus for support?
4. Why did you leave the apostolic church? Explain please.
5. What could the church have done to keep you from leaving the church? Explain please.
6. Do you feel that you will one day come back to the apostolic church? Explain please.
7. Has anyone from the church reached out to you by phone, text, Facebook, or any other social media since you left the church?

8. Do you visit the church for special events? How often?
9. Have you switched from Christianity to another religion? Why?
10. Do you have any comments or suggestions for the church leaders?

Findings collected from the participants who answered the questions to part 2 of the survey questionnaire were intense. The total number of participants was thirty-five. The comments from the young people cast blame on the traditions of the church, pastoral doctrine, treatment from church members and their parents, which they said contributed to them leaving the church. However, there were some young people who did not leave the Apostolic faith, they just left the church that they were attending. The author provided direct quotes submitted voluntarily and honestly by the respondents that they expressed as a concern or hindrance to them remaining in the church. Their answers to the questions were typed in the space provided on the survey that the researcher copied verbatim into this document. Participants had the liberty to type in their answers to the questions without bias on the part of the researcher. Security measures were in place from Survey Monkey to protect the participants' responses. Just for clarity, the researcher could not alter the respondents answers nor did she desire to do so. Again, the researcher did not have direct contact with the respondents who completed this survey questionnaire. The names of all the participants referred to the researcher and their identity on the survey was anonymous. There were apparently several areas of vulnerability and brokenness acknowledged by the teenagers and young adults who took time to participate in this research study. It is the researcher's hope those resolutions can be obtained going forward that will repair fractured relationships between the young people and the church.

Questions to part 2 of the survey were answered by participants with a yes or no answer. While other answers were one or two sentences or a short narrative on the participant's life experiences. This researcher felt that the voices of the youth were important and chose to quote their responses and perspectives in their own words.

Therefore, answers in this section could not be analyzed in percentages as in part 1 of the survey.

Question 1. What was the most difficult thing for you being in an Apostolic church? The answers provided detailed "not being able to wear pants, jewelry, and nail polish. Did not fit in with the church members. Length of the services were too long. People in the church were too judgmental. Restriction of activities outside the church such as we couldn't go to proms, parties, or sports games. The church had cliques and show favoritism. Felt that the material in the church was outdated and irrelevant to modern day living. And church was boring" to them.

Question 2. While at college were you able to find a church and go to it?

This question was answered by thirty-four respondents; one did not answer the question. The answers were comprised of twelve nos, twelve yeses, and nine N/As.

Question 3. Were you able to meet other Christians on campus for support?

This question was answered by thirty-five respondents. The answers were eleven nos, seventeen yeses, and eight N/As.

Questions 4. Why did you leave the apostolic church? Explain please.

Respondent 1 documented that "I was bullied by the members and leaders. Church leaders and members killed my spirit and impacted my faith." He stated that "the treatment became so harsh that I left the church and moved to another state." He also stated, "It was when I left the environment that I realized how imbalanced and unhealthy I was. I allowed the church to consume me altogether. I was an ordained deacon...I will never be a deacon again."

Respondent 2 stated that "the church pastor was crooked and hungry for money."

Respondent 3 stated, "I felt alone and didn't want anybody close to me."

Respondent 4 stated, "Church was not a necessary part of my life."

Respondent 5 stated, "I left the church because in order for me to get the best understanding of life I needed to learn from many different lifestyles and perspectives. I wanted a broader insight into what the human experience entailed."

Respondent 6 stated, "I had a child and the pastor told me to apologize. I disagreed and never went back."

Respondent 7 stated, "Because the picture is bigger than church—it's about your relationship with God."

Respondent 8 stated, "I was hurt by the leader and silenced while the others were doing the same things as me and they were not silenced- it was favoritism."

Respondent 10 stated, "My pastor would not answer specific questions that the young people wanted answers to."

Respondent 13 stated, "I didn't feel the apostolic church provided a safe space for young people to candidly talk about their issues and ask questions about the Bible."

Respondent 17 stated, "I didn't have the motivation anymore."

Respondent 18 stated, "The church and I had difference in beliefs."

Respondent 21 stated, "Mentally, I left for a while."

Respondent 22 stated, "I worked a lot during the week and rested on Sundays."

Respondent 26 stated, "One of my leaders passed away."

Respondent 28 stated, "I was getting bad vibes from the members."

Respondent 30 stated, "I didn't feel comfortable."

Respondent 31 stated, "The church was too rigid in giving young people the opportunity to experience life. Everything is not a sin."

Respondent 34 stated, "The messages became rooted in politics and didn't provide true explanation."

Question 5. What could the church have done to keep you from leaving the church? Please explain.

Respondent 1 stated, "The church could have been more loving and kind and held the leaders (bullies) more accountable."

Respondent 3 stated, "I felt like the church was too judgmental."

Respondent 5 stated, "Not sure if anything could have been done. I felt like church was like school and I learned as much as I could from one particular setting. Eventually, it was time to move on to learn from other experiences and ways of thinking."

Respondent 7 stated, "Stop being fake, stop accepting people to the church then talk about them among other members."

Respondent 8 stated, "Stop favoritism."

Respondent 10 stated, "The church could have listened to me without making me always feel like I was wrong."

Respondent 13 stated, "The church could have created a better atmosphere and safe space for those who had questions about the apostolic faith, the Bible and life issues."

Respondent 17 stated, "Encouraged me."

Respondent 18 stated, "The church could have not spoken ill of people that have different values."

Respondent 19 stated, "I wished there were leaders and youth pastors to talk to."

Respondent 20 stated, "Having a good relationship with the pastor and the church members, be friendly instead of cliques and drama."

Respondent 24 stated, "The church could have been more compassionate towards their struggle and not judgmental."

Respondent 26 stated, "The church could have order."

Respondent 28 stated, "Learn to communicate better and not have the whole church know everybody's business."

Respondent 29 stated, "The church could be accepting of homosexuals and acknowledge that we are still God's people, love is not sin."

Respondent 30 stated, "Explain the Bible better and not judge."

Respondent 31 stated, "Learn how to integrate the church with life outside the church."

Respondent 34 stated, "Spoke more of truth instead of politics."

Respondent 35 stated, "Embraced me and could have taught the Word."

Question 6. Do you feel that you will one day come back to the apostolic church?

The answers were fourteen yeses, six nos, seven maybes, and eight respondents stated that they never left the church; total responses were thirty-five.

Question 7. Has anyone from the church reached out to you by phone, text, Facebook, or any other social media since you left the church?

The answers were fourteen nos and nineteen yeses; total responses were thirty-five.

Question 8. Do you visit the church for special events? How often?

The answers were seventeen nos and eighteen yeses—sometimes on holidays; total responses were thirty-five.

Question 9. Have you switched from Christianity to another religion? Why?

The answers were thirty-one nos, two yeses, two N/As.

One of the two respondents who documented that they switched from Christianity stated, "Yes, I feel completely satisfied with my new frame of religion." The other respondent simply stated, "Yes," that they had switched. The total number of responses were thirty-five.

Question 10. Do you have any comments or suggestions for the church leaders? Your voice is important!

The answers were eighteen yeses, eleven nos, two N/As, and four people skipped it; total number respondents were thirty-one.

Respondent 1 stated, "People in leadership should be held accountable for their actions. They should not use their authority to take advantage of or bully people who are timid or new or unlearned. People are hurting and looking for hope. When they come to church, they should not be met with toxin people who get off on power and control."

Respondent 2 stated, "Cater to the youth, hold carnival or cookouts in your neighborhood to allow the community to feel like they have a safe haven."

Respondent 5 stated, "It is important to relate context to young people; include young people in creating events for young people."

Respondent 7 stated, "Stop separating the church from the world."

Respondent 8 stated, "Stay true, stop favoritism in the church."

Respondent 10 stated, "Listen to young people. Sometimes we are forced out or like we sinned so bad we can't come back. Be non-judgmental. We have trauma in our houses and trauma from church. Listen and show you care."

Respondent 12 stated, "Don't be so judgmental. Be more welcoming and react out personally to people that you see struggling spiritually."

Respondent 13 stated, "Create a safe haven for people to be honest about their struggles in faith and life. Become more active in the communities around the church to teach the kids and young adults the importance of giving back."

Respondent 15 stated, "Keep encouraging the youth and young adults."

Respondent 16 stated, "As long as they aren't harming anyone, allow people to express themselves however way they want."

Respondents 19 stated, "The older saints need to be an example of God and his teaching to the young people."

Respondent 20 stated, "Pastors should have a relationship with your members, instead of picking and choosing who to talk to."

Respondent 21 stated, "The youth of today show their love for God through their arts, music, dance, praise, etc. allow space for that. Connect more with other ministries outside of the normal conference so that the youth may be exposed more. Finally, supplement the word with consistent youth and young adult Bible study."

Respondent 24 stated, "One key to keeping youth in the church is making them feel more ownership in the church. Most youth leave because they feel unappreciated, left out, and don't fit in. Get the youth invested in the growth of the growth."

Respondent 25 stated, "Get to know the members."

Respondent 26 stated, "Thankful for new church family."

Respondent 28 stated, "Invest more into the youth. It's not what you say but how you say it."

Summary of the answers rendered here in part 2 by the respondents indicated that the church and the young people had a lot of work to do together to repair damaged relationships. Somehow, the ministries in the churches need to put forth a greater effort to win back the misguided, confused, and lost youth without bombarding them with rules on what they can and cannot do. A display of Christianity is more readily received by young people when they can see it in the individuals that they trust and are around the most. Consider the attraction and work of Jesus Christ; the crowds pushed their way to be near him. He healed their sicknesses and diseases and fed them. In essence, Jesus met their needs first and then he preached the kingdom of God to them (Matthew 15:29–38 KJV).

Interviews with Inactive Youth Members

Informal interviews with three participants were held over the telephone with inactive youth who used to be members of Pentecostal Apostolic churches in the Philadelphia area. Their identity and the name of the churches that they used to attend was not disclosed as promised prior to their interview as part of the condition that they would speak to this researcher. When the participants were asked what was the number one reason that they stopped going to church, they said it was because they had family issues. They felt that their parents were hypocrites. They acted holy at church but when they got home, they acted like the devil.

Interviewee 1

One of the young adults reported that her mother used profanity at her often, and she would lose her temper and fight her with her fists. She said it was hard for her to respect her mother. She said it was pointless to go to church and then come home to chaos. She stated that she left the church, and she left her home from her mother. She stated that she is studying Islam. She does not know if she will come back to church.

Interviewee 2

The second reason given for leaving the church was they wanted to hang out with their friends. One young adult stated that he thought hanging out with his friends was more important than going to church. He commented that he was tired of going to church. He stated that he had made a lot of mistakes trying to fit in with his friends and now he is trying to get his life together: "I know God has been merciful to me." He said that he wants to return to the church but not at this time.

Interviewee 3

This participant verbalized openly his feelings more than the other two interviewees. He stated in his opinion teenagers and young adults are leaving the church because it is a time to try something different. They are trying to fit in with their friends since graduating from school or college. They feel free from restrictions of the church and their parents. "Young people are trying alcohol and wine for the first time, and they're going wild and crazy because the friends that are around them don't tell them to stop and they don't put a limit on them." He said, "A lot of the youth are turning to drinking, smoking, drugs, money, and sex out of curiosity."

He stated, "I feel that the preached word is not registering in the youth's head. They got to experience it and see if they can come out of it—they learn from their failures." He mentioned that "the Bible seems like a story" to him, and he does not fully understand. He added that the sermons should be interesting and relatable to the young people and what their issues are because "a lot of young people don't talk to their parents. They go to their friends for advice and to talk and sometimes they get the wrong information."

He also stated that "young adult males need men who can mentor them like a big brother in the church" since "many fathers are not good examples to their Christian sons" and the "mothers cannot show their sons how to be a man."

Lastly, he pointed out that young people need the church to let them know that they are needed and that they are valued.

The researcher thanked the interviewees for their time and participation in this interview. They were informed that their input would be shared with pastors and youth leaders to improve communication and connectivity between the church and the young people. The goal would be to help young people stay in the church.

Interviews with Pastors Whose Church Closed

Pastor 1 Interviewee

An unnamed pastor, age sixty-eight, who had been a pastor for seventeen years was interviewed. He stated that his congregation dwindled down to only elderly people in attendance for years. Therefore, as the older members died, they were not replaced by younger members. Families that were connected to the older members who had died either belonged to another church or were nonbelievers; some of them used to visit the church from time to time but not lately. When inquired if any of the deceased member's families wanted to remain at the church, he stated that they did not want to stay despite them being raised up in that church. They did not think that the tradition of a family church was important. The congregation had dwindled down to three members, two senior citizens and one member in their fifties. Since no one has been coming to church, he closed the church doors. The pastor does not know if he will reopen the church doors in the future. He had been visiting other churches in his area to meet his spiritual need.

Considering what happened to this church, it is foolish for aged pastors not to mentor and groom younger people to carry on the ministry. It has been said that young people draw young people. All churches need young people for continual growth, diversity, and sustainability. Most young people do not want to be under the pastorate of a senior citizen pastor and especially someone who does not have a vision that includes them in the future. As the scripture says, "Where there is no vision, the people perish" (Proverbs 29:18 KJV).

During a recent drive-by through the Philadelphia and the surrounding communities, there were countless closed small churches predominately in black and Hispanic neighborhoods. There were also small- and middle-sized churches in the suburb neighborhoods outside of Philadelphia who used to have racially mixed congregations that were closed also. The reasons for the closure of those churches were not readily available to this researcher.

Pastor 2 Interviewee

Another pastor aged fifty whose name we did not reveal had pastored a small church with a few young people and a few adults for approximately five years. He stated that the members of the church resented him for correcting them. He said, on one Sunday, he reprimanded the congregation, saying to them that if they did not like it, they could leave so they stood up and left the church. The pastor did not share why he attempted to disciple the congregation nor where the congregation went when they left his church. He said when the people left, he knew that he could not financially maintain it, so he closed the doors and joined an established Apostolic church.

Recognizably, these are changing times and congregations are not committed to one leader and one church for the rest of their lives as in the past. Furthermore, some congregations have issues, and they are troubled churches for pastors to serve from the start. Likewise, some pastors are difficult, domineering, assertive, and arrogant. Sadly, when pastors attempt to control the congregations with fear as in the old days, those tactics do not work in these modern times or with this generation of believers. These two pastors expressed that they experienced an emotional hurt, and they were blamed for the closure of their churches. Pastors should be aware that people today can pick and choose which church they want to attend and if they are not satisfied, they will leave.

Chapter 5

Recommendations and Suggestions to Prevent Teenagers and Young Adults from Leaving the Church

To complete this research study, numerous books and articles on the subject, along with a survey questionnaire and interviews were utilized. There were many reasons documented for young people leaving the church all over the world; however, the focus presented here was concentrated on the United Stated of America. Below are some recommendations and suggestions that could potentially assist the pastors, youth leaders, board of governors, and congregations with their efforts to retain, reclaim, and prevent teenagers and young adults from existing the church. These recommendations and suggestions may not be feasible or applicable for every house of worship. Therefore, they will need to be reshaped, reframed, adjusted, and applied accordingly to fit the local church's strategy and administration.

According to *The Washington Post*, an article written by Powell, Mulder, and Griffin (2016), "Opinion: To attract young people to your church, you've got to be warm. Not cool." These authors reported that statistics were compiled from 250 congregations and 1,300 young churchgoers ages fifteen to twenty-nine that they had spoken to. The article revealed that young people do not expect to be engaged in a lot of activities at church to keep them busy. They basically want a "warm" church and not a "cool" one. They desired to be active and around loving, caring, sincere, welcoming adults. People who care as much about their physical well-being as they do about the saving of their souls. They are not interested in new gadgets, horns, or whistles as the term goes; for them authenticity and simplicity are the attractions to attending church.

This researcher posed recommendations and suggestions in a question-and-answer format for clarity and ease of review from multiple resources:

How to Engage Young People in Worship Services

To keep young people interested in coming to church, it was recommended that congregations redesign their worship services to engage young people in every service not just once a month on youth Sundays. Young people can be paired with their parents, grandparents, or older adults, "so youth can learn from their elders' dedication and older people can be inspired by youthful enthusiasm" (Powell et al. 2016).

To increase teenagers and young adult engagement, worship services could be moved outside the church walls. Worship and praise services could be held in the parking lot of the church, on the streets near the church, at a mall, in a school gymnasium, or a hotel. It could attract teenagers, young adults, and men who do not want to come inside a church, it would be an informal invitation for them to be a part of the service.

A youth band of musicians could be responsible for providing energetic praise and worship songs instead of slow traditional hymns. A lot of the young people do not know the church hymnals, so to inspire them to learn them, an agreement could be negotiated between the senior music director and the youth band. With this agreement, the youth band could set up rehearsals at the church and prepare to play on certain Sundays and special occasions. It is believed that this activity will motivate the youth to invite the family and friends to see them perform and hopefully spark an interest in them to continue to come and participate in the church.

Whenever and wherever young people are viewed as essential members of the congregation, they can learn effectively by interactive engagement and hands-on participation. Studies have shown that young churchgoers' participation at church did encourage other young people to attend church. As the old saying goes, "Young people draw young people."

Why Is Mentorship Important in the Church?

Mentorship programming invites young people to grow by teaching their peers and others. It also provides an opportunity for the elderly members in the church to teach and to be role models to the younger generation. Sessions can be held structurally at the church in an open and safe environment. It can be peer to peer or side by side with a young person and an older person. When young people are paired with an older member in the church, it can create an intergenerational cohesiveness and connectivity that would close the gap between the old and the young. Mentorship is an effective way to grow disciples for Christ.

To attract young and older people for the mentorship program, an announcement could be broadcasted from the pulpit that invites volunteers who have time to commit themselves to working in small groups. Those interested could meet at the church or a designated community center with approval from the parents weekly for six to eight weeks for one hour to one and a half hour. The meetings suggested by Ed Springer (2023), "The three *Ss* of youth mentoring—Youthworks" need to be "safe, simple, structured" and maintain consistency so that the mentors and mentees will know what to expect when they meet. The mentors would observe a set agenda that was planned in advance of their meetings so it would allow the mentees to include their specific topics of interests. It would also be a perfect time for the youth to discuss their issues and receive proper support from spiritual leaders. The goal for mentorship would be to help the mentees grow in their preferred area of interest to enrich their lives first then benefit the church and community.

As the church prepares and move into the future, it is important that teenagers and young adults be trained as missionaries, evangelists, ministers, deacons, ushers, Sunday school and Bible class teachers, program coordinators, musical directors, and other essential ministries to keep the church operational and alive. Many of the older saints are not well, and some of them are having difficulty with their mobility and it would be a pleasure for them to have a younger person accompanying them and assisting regularly in the work of the Lord. Most young people stated in the research survey that they wanted to feel needed and valued. Overtime, mentorship grooms the youth to be future leaders in the church and community. It promotes a sense of pride and ownership for them in the church.

Why Incorporate Financial Budget for the Youth?

Another excellent idea from the authors of *The Washington Post* article "To Attract Young People to Your Church, You've Got to Be Warm, Not Cool" (Powell, Mulder, and Griffin 2016) was for the church to financially set aside funds for "meal budgets" where small groups of young people with volunteer leaders come and have a meal together. Perhaps they could meet every three months to discuss current trends and concerns that they are facing at home, at school, in the community. Their meetings would help them to "warm up," bond and communicate safely with each other.

Teenagers and young adults stated in the research survey that some of them left the church because their friends were not attending. Whenever possible, the church can arrange and sponsor sports activities like baseball, basketball, roller skating, swimming, and board games where the young people can invite their family and friends to come and participate. Sometimes young people want to come to church, but they do not have the money to pay for certain activities so having a budget set aside for the youth will cover those young people who are indigent. Through friendly and welcoming extension of kindness, young people can look forward to making new friends and reconnect with the old ones in a Christian atmosphere. The goal is to reach the unchurched and reclaim those kids that have left the church.

We cannot forget those teenagers and young adults who have not left the church, they need encouragement also. With the financial budget in place, the church could arrange a special program or banquet to recognize and celebrate young people who are in the church, those who are participating in specific capacities and departments; likewise, those who have accomplished educational and career goals. To demonstrate to the youth that they are important, essential, and valuable to their churches, the church could award them financial scholarships, certificates, trophies, plaques, and gift cards in the presence of their family and friends.

Again, as stated by the respondents on the research study questionnaire, teenagers and young people implied that if they had been shown in some way that they were appreciated and valued, they would not have left the church. We desire teenagers and young people to remain in the church and be happy serving the Lord so as often as the church budget will allow, the youth will need to be recognized and acknowledged in some small way.

Why Modern Technology in the Church?

Young people are skilled in technology and social media platforms. And they can assist the church to revamp the brochures, literature, tracks, and cataloging sermons for spotlighting the church at its location in the community. Most youth are familiar with computers and graphic design from their first educational experience in kindergarten to graduation from college. The church has progressed from just having worship service and classes inside the church to having it virtually viewed over the internet by thousands of people at one time. Young people are remarkable in their thinking outside of the box and participation by networking with other systems. They can assist part-time, full-time, or seasonally according to their availability at the church. It has been noted by Darby's article (2021) "8 Ways to connect young adults to the church" was to credit their contribution to the church, it can motivate them to stay in the church, boost their self-esteem, and make them feel valued.

The use of technology and the internet are increasing more and more incrementally as means of communication to contact members, schedule meetings, collect funds, post announcements, attend virtual educational/spiritual classes, pray for those sick and hospitalized, and et cetera.

Teenagers and young people can reach out to other teenagers and young people and invite them to church activities and assess how they are doing over time. They can reach out to their friends and invite them to attend special services that are scheduled at the church and the church can provide refreshments.

Young people can assist in setting up and participating on the Prayer Line as youth intercessors for children that call into a toll-free prayer line. This will help them to give back to the community and train them to evangelize for Jesus. Some teenagers and young people can assist other students by tutoring academic classes online using the church website. It can motivate some of them that participate to become educators as well as decrease boredom. With competent, knowledgeable individuals to manage the church's communication through modern technology, it will not fall behind.

Why New Member Classes?

Individuals who have had the opportunity to attend new member classes reported that they gained confidence knowing the pastor's vision for the church. They also acquired knowledge and understanding of the church's mission, policy, procedures, program agendas, and what was their financial expected obligations in the church. They were able to get to know some of the other potential members of the congregation and their interests. In the class, they were taught the doctrine of the church and were encouraged to ask questions on anything that pertained to the church's beliefs. They were encouraged to participate in activities of their interests and invited to share their expertise to improve the image and services in the church.

Establishment of new member classes for teenagers, young adults, and adults in the late 1990s was an effective way of discipleship, and it is believed to be necessary today and in the future for the retention and sustainability of the church congregation. A new member class could initially be taught by the pastor and then handed off to one of the young adults to teach. It should be taught by someone who is well familiar with the church's history and has already completed the new member class. New member classes could be offered as a one-time three-hour class on a Sunday afternoon after morning service, or a ninety-minute class over a two-week period, or once a month or quarterly as appropriate to the church influx and list of potential new members. Thom S. Rainer (1999) in "High Expectations: The Remarkable Secret for Keeping People in Your Church" stated that if a church requires potential members to take the new member class, it may lose some member, but if it does not have a new member class it surely will lose potential members since they do not know the church or what is expected of them.

Why Is Church Protocol Important?

It is stated in scripture that everything should be done decently and in order (1 Corinthians 14:40 KJV). The behavior and administration of some churches are a real turnoff to visitors and potential members of all ages. Church protocol should adhere to etiquette and show reverence to the Lord Jesus Christ while honoring the authorities of the church, the church members, and the visitors who come into the church. Protocol is defined as "a code of courtesies, proper practices, set of rules regarding church worship service" according to Elder Demetrius C. Moye (2012) at C. H. Mason District from "Church Protocol and Etiquette."

During this research study, inappropriate and dysfunctional behaviors were identified and found offensive to teenagers, young adults, and adult men who had left the church. Some young people reported on the survey questionnaire such improper behaviors as the preachers calling out their names in their sermons that identified them as having had committed some act of sin. Claimed by author

David Murrow (2005), *Why Men Hate Church*, stated that several men pointed out that they were bombarded by pastors, ministers, and altar worker grabbing and touching on them in their prayer lines. These men stated they were most uncomfortable and felt their space was invaded.

When most people to come church, they are seeking spirituality and a good experience. So an established and execution of proper church protocol for all participants in the church ministries will decrease the occurrence of unhappy experiences and complaints from people who may enter for worship. Each ministry at the church should be required to attend a class or workshop at the church or at a religious organizational conference so that all servants of Christ will know what to do, how to act toward the churched and unchurched, know what is expected of them, and all paid staff and all volunteers should be trained on the same subject matter and process. If a church does not have the necessary literature or resources to set up church protocol training, the internet is a good source that can guide church leaders on how to set up church protocol for various departments in their churches. Most of the time, instructional information can be downloaded for free from many online sites and copied for continued education purposes. Compliance to an established church protocol will attract new potential members; potential new members are looking for ministries that are well organized and are welcoming to visitors. All churches must keep in mind that the first impression to visitors is a lasting impression. And depending on how the visitors are greeted and treated at the door will determine if they return again to the church.

What Are the Benefits of Attending Church?

There are significant benefits to attending church that most people do not think about until they are in the midst of distress, sickness or trouble, or some life-altering situation. An article written by Dawn Klinge (2017) provided "10 Unexpected Benefits of Church." I believe that this article not only reminds the believer of unexpected benefits of attending church, but they are truly words of inspiration to invite teenagers, young adults, and men to come back to church. These ten unexpected benefits provide an extraordinary description of what a good thriving supportive church should look like and do for the attendee.

1. "Church provides social support."

    Attending church on regular basis or staying at a church depends on how people are treated and how they get along with each other. It is an opportunity to be in a spiritual environment separated from worldliness with like-minded people. Frequent attendance and encounters with friendly members at church generally will forge relation-ships. Good relationships among the congregation have coined the phrase "church family." Having a loving and caring "church family" provides social, mental, and spiritual support to individuals and families inside the circle of brothers and sisters in Christ. Some people have reported that they are treated better by their "church family" than they are by the natural family. The Bible describes the exemplary conduct of the believer toward another believer, "As we have therefore the opportunity, let us do good unto all men, especially unto them who are of the household of faith" (Galatians 6:10 KJV). Also attending church helps teenagers and young adults meet people who have the same interests, concerns, and common goals in life as they do. It can lead to many positive pathways such as in employment/career, education, health, and ministry. Social connections made at church have been known to last for many years.

2. "People who go to church are healthier."

    It is believed that being brought up in the church and listening constantly to the Word of God has influenced the saints on how they ought to take care of their body and health. The believers' body is the temple of the Lord. As a result, believers avoid over consumption of food, drink, and other indulgences which has preserved and maintained the integrity of their overall health status.

We cannot dismiss the fact that prayer has kept many young and old from ill health and death. The church encourages churchgoers to pray and fast because it cleanses the mind and body of toxins. As believers, we depend on the Lord Jesus for healing even when we take prescribed medications and submit to medical treatments. We are assured that it is God's will that we be in good health. Otherwise, it is difficult to serve God with a diseased and sick body. Therefore, we must all strive to remain healthy with good nutrition and exercise to the glory of God.

3. "Church provides an opportunity to connect with God."

The entrance into a church automatically informs us that the atmosphere and environment is different from that being at home, school, or work. Being at church is a place where the spirit of God dwells, and it allows us to be in his presence. It is a time where we can speak to God personally from our hearts. We can tell him thank you for all that he has done for us, and we can freely tell him all about our problems without him criticizing us. We can ask him to forgive us of our sins. How wonderful it is to know that God is near us, and He hears our prayers. We must continue to pray and be intercessors for the teenagers and young adults. Many souls have returned to Christ because somebody prayed for them at the altar.

4. "Church helps strengthen marriages."

According to the author, she reported that a study done by a sociologist at the University of Virginia, couples who attend church together are happier than those who not and they statistically had less divorces. The bond of matrimony grew stronger among couples of the same faith when compared to those whose spouses were of different faith. Sermons that spotlight the relationship of the church espoused to Christ supports marriage. Married believers can pray, fast, read the Word, and fellowship together, which increases their spirituality and love for each other and their family.

5. "Church helps us give back."

Most churches are cognizant of the need to give to their local communities through food pantries, clothing drives, book bags with school supplies, barbering and cosmetology services. The young people have stated that it was so rewarding to them to see the little kids and families come to their events and receive charitable donations. As the dip in the economy has affected many, it is important for the church to continue to inspire young people to volunteer their time and services in assisting those who are less fortunate than they are with whatever they can appropriately contribute. After all it is about loving our neighbors as ourselves.

6. "Church reminds us of our identity."

Gathering at the church reminds us of the horrific price Christ paid on Calvary's cross for our redemption. It is vital to remember that we were created for purpose and pleasure. Everything that we say and do reflects our identity to Christ. The Bible tells us to let our light so shine that men may see our good works and glorify the father in heaven (Matthew 5:15–16 KJV). We are his sons and daughters because we have his name, and we do not want to shame him.

7. "People who go to church suffer less depression."

A study was conducted by the University of Saskatchewan where the "incidence of depression was 22% lower among people who went to church." Going to church is also beneficial in lowering stress because worshipping and praising God brings comfort and an elevation of the spirit to trust God to meet our every need. In the presence of God is peace and safety as confirmed through the word of the psalmist David, "You will show me the path of life; In your presence is fulness of joy; At Your right hand are pleasures forevermore" (Psalm 16:11 NKJV).

8. "Church reminds us of a deeper meaning to life."

Attending church and hearing the Word of God reminds us that we are temporary dwellers here on earth, this is not our permanent home. Our lives are like a vapor that will soon dissipate. While we are alive, we must spend our days serving the Lord and witnessing to others to let them know that the Lord is coming back one day for a people who have lived righteously in this world. There is no guarantee that everyone will reach old age; therefore, the message of salvation should be shared with every living soul.

9. "Church promotes accountability and routine."

Churchgoers and visitors respond better to churches who have established routines in place from the order of services down to scheduled activities for children. Accountability and routine eliminate confusion and disorder.

The church teaches that we are accountable to our local assemblies and each other. It encourages reliability, dependability, and faithfulness to our commitment to serve in God's house, "Let all things be done decently and in order" (1 Corinthians 14:40 KJV) as not to hinder the unbeliever.

Accountability and routine are precursors to skills learned in time management. They also enable children to be prepared in advance for scheduled activities. Accountability and routines are essential tools in the box of life.

10. "Church helps us learn about forgiveness."

At church, when the Word of God is preached, it convicts our hearts to ask God to forgive us of our sins and wrong doings, it allows us to forgive ourselves and to forgive those who have hurt and wronged us. God's word softens our hearts and fills our mouths with pleasant words. Because it reminds us of God's great grace and mercy toward us. For we all have sinned, and we must not look down on sinners. Sinners young and old need to know that God loves them, and He will forgive them of their sins if they ask Him.

Chapter 6

Conclusion

At the closure of this research study, there were many factors revealed that contributed to teenagers and young adults from ages eighteen to twenty-nine, leaving or have left the Christian church. Unfortunately, there was not just one specific reason or cause uncovered from participants who completed the survey questionnaire provided by the researcher or the many authors and other researchers of this subject. Reportedly, the decline in the number of young people attending church has progressively worsened over the last twenty to thirty years. It has reached a global proportion and awareness to religious leaders and especially the small Pentecostal Apostolic churches. The impact is seen all over of young people who have walked away from their roots in Christianity. Their departure from the church is affecting the growth and sustainability of the church for future generations.

Parents are not attending church with their children as they once did in the past. Lifeway Research data showed in the article "Most Teenagers Drop Out of Church as Young Adults," 66% of the young people stated that they had life changing events in their life that caused them to stop attending church. As a result, we are seeing this new generation growing up without having the knowledge of God and a relationship with Jesus Christ due to their parents not being interested in going to church. They have stated that church was not relevant in their lives. Many teenagers and young adults after completion of high school, entrance and graduation from college have forsaken the teachings of the Pentecostal Apostolic church to create their own sense of spirituality, or they have embraced philosophies and teachings of non-Christian beliefs like Islam.

The research showed from the survey respondents that teenagers and young adults left the church because they felt unloved, unappreciated, unrecognized, and devalued by their spiritual leaders and the congregations that they tried to connect to. It has been recommended that for churches to grow in these modern times, it will have to adapt to the rapid changes evolving through technology and the new ways of having church to survive the challenges at hand. Teenagers and young adults will have to be trained and included in the planning, execution, and functionality of the church services and administration in preparation for the future. Establishment of new member classes was found to improve the attendance of the members who completed the classes. Actively involved young people will learn from intergenerational members and inspire other young people to attend church.

Teenagers and young adults expressed that are looking for a warm church with pastors, youth leaders, and congregations that they can connect with emotionally, physically, and spiritually. They want to have the opportunity to serve in the house of the Lord and freely ask questions relating to their life experiences and situations without being criticized or condemned. The church is expected to move forward into the future, but the growth of the church is predicated on how well teenagers and young adults are received, welcomed, and appropriately trained. Timely interactive-enculturation education and training of the present-day young people who have not left the church should assist the church in making disciples as the scriptures has charge the church to do. Will these recommendations and suggestions in this research study facilitate the growth of the church in the future and prevent the youth from leaving or motivate those teenagers and young adults who have left to return? We do not know; only time will tell.

Appendices

A. Letter to the Pastors

B. Letter to Inactive Youths

C. Survey Questionnaire

Letter to the Pastors

February 12, 2021

Dear Pastor or Youth Leader:

I pray that all is well with you, your family, and your congregation. My name is Dorothy Oden. I serve as pastor alongside my husband, Bishop Gerald Oden at Mt. Zion Apostolic Church in Philadelphia, Pennsylvania. I am writing to you for your assistance as I complete the process towards obtaining my PhD in Theology at Parkersburg Bible College. My thesis seeks to investigate and discover possible reasons for the steady decline in the number of teenagers and young adults who are or were **18 to 29 years old** when they graduated from high school or college, and they stop attending our Christian churches and especially our Pentecostal-Apostolic churches.

I am asking you for a list of ten or more names and addresses or emails of teenagers and young adults that I can mail or email my survey to. The survey does not have any personal identifying information of the participant on it. It is anonymous! The survey is to be returned to me in a postage paid self-addressed envelope or it can be completed on-line.

The answers from the survey will be complied, analyzed, and kept private for my research purpose only and afterward the names and addresses that you provide to me will be deleted from my record. **The survey is titled "Teenagers and Young Adults", it is two pages** and should take about ten minutes or less to complete. The survey is available online at these two links:

https://www.surveymonkey.com/r/FKGH9LM and
https://www.surveymonkey.com/r/FVKGC8J

It is my goal to share the findings of the survey with those pastors and youth leaders who respond to this letter. I anticipate that this survey will provide valuable feedback which can be implemented in our churches as an effort to retain and God willing prevent teenagers and young adults from abandoning their Christian faith and leaving the church.

Thank you for your attention and participation in this very important matter. If you have any questions, please feel free to contact me at 215-280-4690; email address: Mtzfirstlady@aol.com.

Sincerely yours in Christ Jesus,

Dorothy Oden
Enclosed: 1 Survey Questionnaire

Letter to Inactive Youths

February 12, 2021

Dear Friend:

I pray that this letter finds you and your family in good health. I am Dorothy Oden. I pastor alongside my husband Bishop Gerald Oden at Mt. Zion Apostolic Church in Philadelphia, Pennsylvania. I am writing to you as a doctorate candidate for my PhD in Theology at Parkersburg Bible College. My thesis focuses on research to explore and explain why young people are leaving the Apostolic churches.

I have been concerned for some time over the steady decline in the number of teenagers and young adults attending our Pentecostal Apostolic churches. As you have seen yourself how many young people who after completing high school, enter and graduate from college rarely come to church on Sunday or they have stopped coming to church all together.

I reached out to pastors and youth leaders to obtain a list of teenagers and young adults that I could mail this survey to and I was given your name and address. First, I want to reassure you that only your answers from the survey will be used in my research project. Secondly, the survey is anonymous, and it does not have any personal identifying markers on it. It should only take about ten minutes or less to complete.

I am asking you to please complete the **two-page survey** and mail it back to me in the postage paid self-addressed envelope or go online and take the survey. It is titles, **"Teenagers and Young Adults"** at https://www.surveymonkey.com/r/FKGH9LM and https://www.surveymonkey.com/r/FVKGC8J

Your responses are truly needed, valued, and appreciated as an effective way to improve the growth of our churches. It will be a blessing to me as I work to finish my research project. Thank you very much for your quick response in completing this survey and returning it to me.

Best regards,
Dorothy Oden
Enclosed: 1 Survey Questionnaire

Survey Questionnaire

Teenagers and Young Adults—Survey Part 1

Please answer the questions below as honestly as possible. It is anonymous!!!

1. Were you born and raised in the apostolic church that you attended?
   - o Yes
   - o No
2. Which did you attend?
   - o Sunday School Classes
   - o Bible Classes
   - o None
3. Did the church have New Member Classes for new members?
   - o Yes
   - o No
4. Were the members of the church friendly?
   - o Yes
   - o No
   - o Sometimes
5. How would you rate your relationship with the pastor(s) and church leaders?
   - o Poor
   - o Fair
   - o Good
   - o Excellent

6. What need did the church help you with? Check all that apply
   - o Transportation
   - o Financial Hardship
   - o Health Issues
   - o Spiritual
   - o Other

7. Please select the reason(s) you do not attend church.
   - o Was offended by someone in the church
   - o Had a difficult time fitting in with others
   - o Church was boring
   - o Have to work on the weekends

8. Was the teaching and preaching of the Bible clear to you?
   - o Yes
   - o No

9. Did you participate on any of the following? Check all that apply.
   - o Praise Team / Choir / Music Ministry
   - o Youth & Young Adult Ministry
   - o Usher Board / Hospitality
   - o None

10. Did you feel safe at church?
    - o Yes
    - o No

Teenagers and Young Adults—Survey Part 2

1. What was the most difficult thing for you being in an Apostolic church?

   ____

2. While at college were you able to find a church and go to it?

   ____

3. Were you able to meet with other Christians on campus for support?

   ____

4. Why did you leave the apostolic church? Explain please

   ____

5. What could the church have done to keep you from leaving the church? Explain please

   ____

6. Do you feel that you will one day come back to the Apostolic church? Explain please

   ____

7. Has anyone from the church reached out to you by phone, text, Facebook, or any other social media since you left the church?

   ____

8. Do you visit the church for special events? How Often?

   ____

9. Have you switched from Christianity to another religion? Why?

   ____

10. Do you have any comments or suggestions for the church leaders? Your voice is important!

____

Thank you for completing this survey and returning it to me!

Reference List

Barna. "Three Spiritual Journeys of Millennials." Barna Group. June 3, 2013. Barna.org/research/three-spiritual-journeys-of-millennials/#.VvGPTMdOL8s.

Barna. "Six Reasons Young Christians Leave Church." Barna Group. September 27, 2011. www.barna.com/research/six-reasons-young-christians-leave-church/.

Barna. "What Young Adults say Is Missing from Church." Barna Group. December 16, 2020. https://www.barna.com/research/missing-church/

Bernard, David K. 2001. *Growing A Church—Seven Apostolic Principles*. Hazelwood, MO: Word Aflame Press, 9–273.

Bowen, Alison. "How to raise a child in an interfaith marriage." *Chicago Tribune*, March 17, 2016. https://www.chicagotribune.com>lifestyles>parenting.

Brouwer, Wayne. "Here's What the Local Church Will Look Like in 20 Years." July 15, 2021. Church Leadership Center. https://churchleadershipcenter.org/heres-local-church-will-look-like-in-20-years/.

Bruce, Debra F. "Teen Depression." June 22, 2020, www.webmd.com.

COBUILD Advanced English Dictionary. Copyright © HarperCollins Publishers, 1987, https://www.collinsdictionary.com.

Cox, Daniel and Amelia Thomson-DeVeaux. "Millennials Are Leaving Religion And Not Coming Back." December 12, 2019. https://fivethirtyeight.com/features/millennials-are-leaving-religion-and-not-coming-back/.

Curry, Michael B. 2020. *Love Is the Way—Holding on to Hope in Troubling*
Times. New York: Avery, 1–259.

Earls, Aaron. "Most Teenagers Drop Out of Church as Young Adults." LifeWay Research. January 15, 2019. https://lifewayresearch.com/2019/01/15/most-teenagers-drop-out-of-church-as-young-adults/.

Emba, Christian. "Why millennials are skipping church and not going back." *The Washington Post*. October 27, 2019. www.washingtonpost.com.

Fletcher, Mal. "Holographic, automation and digital debt: 6 ways the Church will look different in 2040." December 12, 2019. https://www.premierchristianity.com/home/holographics-automation-and -digital-debt-6-ways-the-church-will-look-different-in-2040/1514.article.

French, Ryan A. "4 Problems Preacher's Kids Face." A Pentecostal Blog & Apostolic Voice Podcast. May 31, 2021. https://ryanafrench.com>author.

Gibson, Tim. "Engage & Grow: How to attract young people to your church." December 17, 2020. https://blog.churchdesk.com/how-to-attract-young-people-to-your-church.

Harrison, Mike. "Christian College Students Face Challenges at Public Universities." Great Lakes Christian College. May 17, 2018. https://blog.glcc.edu.

Henderson, Joyce T. 2001. *How to Reverse This Trend Youth Leaving the Church*. Xulon Press, 1–165.

Holy Bible. 2013. New Living Translation. Carol Stream, Illinois, Tyndale Publisher.

Jabbari, Bahareh and Audra S. Rouster. "Family Dynamics"—StatPearls—NCBI Bookshelf. July 27, 2020 https://www.ncbi.nim.nih.gov>books.

Jones, Darby. "8 Ways to connect young adults to the church." January 29, 2021. https://www.resourceums.org/en/content8-ways-tp-connect-young-adults-to-the-church.

Jones, Jeffrey M. "U.S. Church Membership Down Sharply in Past Two Decades." *Gallup*. April 18, 2019. https://news.gallup.

com/poll248837/church-membership-down-sharply-past-two-decades.aspx. 1–12.

Kamenetz, Anya. "The Pandemic Has Researchers Worried About Teen Suicide." *Morning Edition.* September 10, 2020. www.npr.org.

Kinnaman, David. 2011. *You Lost Me. Why Young Christians Are Leaving Church…and Rethinking Faith.* Grand Rapids, MI: Baker Books, 9–249.

Klinge, Dawn. "10 Unexpected Benefits of Church." https://www.crosswalk.com > article.

Krejcir, Richard. 2007. "Statistics and Reasons for Church Decline." www.churchleadership.org/apps/articles/default.asp?articleid=42346.

Simpson, Amy. "Reforming the Church's Response to Mental Illness" Interview with Brianna Lantz. May 25, 2018. https://nation-media.org/mental-illness-church/.

Lizardy-Hajbi, Kristina. 2015. "Engaging Young Adults." American Congregations. Center for Analytics, Research and Data United Church of Christ. www.FaithCommunitiesToday.org.

McGibbon, Karen Harris. "The Psychology of a Double Life." Updated on December 17, 2018. https://www.drkaymc.com/post/the-psychology-of-a-double-life.

Merriam-Webster Dictionary. "Abortifacient." https://www.meriam-webster.com/dictionary/abortifacient.

Merriam-Webster Dictionary. "Infanticide." https://www.meriam-webster.com/dictionary/infanticide.

Meyer, Holly. "Young adults are dropping out of church in large numbers, survey finds. This is why." *USA Today.* December 16, 2020. www.usatoday.com/story/news/nation/2019/01/15why-young-adults-drop-out-church-survey/2580829002/.

Morin, Amy. "Top 10 Social Issues Teens Struggle with Today. Technology Has Changed or Amplified the Struggles Young People Face." June 24, 2020. https://www.verywellfamily.com/startling-facts-about-todays-teenagers-2608914.

Mosher, Jennifer H. 2017. "Then and Now: Early Christianity's Radical Reshaping of Childhood," Praxis 16, no. 3: 1–6.

Moye, Demetrius C. "Church Protocol and Etiquette." C. H. Mason District, April 14, 2012. http://files.snappages.site.

Murphy, Caryle. "Interfaith marriage is common in US, particularly among the recently wed." June 2, 2015. https://www.pewresearch.org.

Murrow, David. 2005. *Why Men Hate Going to Church*. Nashville, TN: Thomas Nelson, 1–232.

Nelson, Thomas. 1982. New King James Version. Copyright.

New International Version. 1997. Wheaton, Illinois: Tyndale House Publishers.

Newcomb, Alyssa. "Pastor Rick Warren's Son Matthew Commits Suicide After lifelong." April 6, 2013. https://abcnews.go.com >story.

Newport, Frank. "Why Are Americans Losing Confidence in Organized Religion?" *Gallup*. July 16, 2019. https://news.gallup.com/opinion/polling-matters/260738/why-americans-losing-confidence-organized-religion.aspx. 1–5.

Jacobs, Pastor Jeff. 2020. "What's Missing in Church." Shepherd Road Presbyterian Church. PastorJeff@Shepherdroad.com.

Pew Research Center. "The Future of World Religions: Population Growth Projections, 2010-2050." April 2, 2015. https://www.pewforum.org/2015/04/02/religious-projections-2010-2050. 1–18.

Pfeiffer, Charles F., Howard F. Vos, John Rea. 1999. *Wycliffe Bible Dictionary*. Hendrickson Publication, 350.

Phillips, Todd. "How NOT to Lead a Double Life." YouTube. July 2, 2016. http://toddphillips.com/how-not-to-lead-a-double-life/.

Pope, Charles. "Marriage and Family at the Time of Jesus." March 26, 2017. Blog.adw.org.

Powell, Kara, Jake Mulder, and Brad Griffin. "Opinion: To attract young people to your church, you've got to be warm. Not cool." *The Washington Post*. September 6, 2016, https://www.washingtonpost.com/news/acts-of-faith/wp/2016/09/06to-attract-young-people-to-your-church-youve-got-tobe-warm-not-cool/.

Rainer, Thom S. 1999. *High Expectations: The Remarkable Secret for Keeping People in Your Church*. Nashville, TN: Broadman and Holman.

Joseph, Ruben. 2011. *Why Are the Young People Leaving the Church? What We Need To Do To Keep Them In.* Xlibris, 1–79.

Russell, Michael F. and Amy Wall. 2004. *The Everything Christianity Book.* Avon, MA: Adams Media, 11.

Smith, William. 1986. *Smith's Bible Dictionary.* Thomas Nelson, 494.

Springer, Ed. "The three Ss of youth mentoring—Youthworks." https://youthworks.net> articles

Stonestreet, John and Morris, Shane. "Why Young People Leave the Church And Why They Stay." January 7, 2020. https://breakpoint.org.

Stringfellow, Alan B. 2014. *Through the Bible in One Year.* Whitaker House. www.whitakerhouse.com.

Williams, Jamaal. "The Stigma Around Mental Illness for Christians." Geneva College Blog. December 17, 2018. https://www.geneva.edu/blog/uncategorized/stigma-mental-illness.

Vanderbloemen. "11 Things a Pastor's Kid May Be Thinking—That You May Not Even Realize," August 22, 2018. https://www.vanderloemen.com/blog/understand-pastors-kid.

Weiss, Kenneth J. "Psychiatry's Ancient Origins," Group for the Advancement of Psychiatry. *Psychiatric Times* 35, no. 11. November 29, 2018. www.psychchiatrictimes.com>view.

Westerhoff III, John H. 2012. *Will Our Children Have Faith?* (third ed.). Morehouse Publishing, 1–88.

Wikipedia, The Free Encyclopedia, https://en.m.wikipedia.org>wiki.

Wilkinson, Bruce H., Paula A. Kirk, and John W. Hoover. 1997. *The Daily Walk Bible.* Tyndale House Publishers.

Wilson, Bill. "What will we see less of and more of in America's churches in the 2020s?" https://baptistnews.com/article/what-will-we-see-less-of-and-more-of-in-americas-churches-in-the-2020s/#.YO-VTC1h1N0.

Your Dictionary. "Blended family." https://www.yourdictionary.com>b.

Zehnder, Zach. "10 Bold Predictions About The Future Church in America." August 5, 2020. https://redletterchallenge.com/10-bold-preditions-about-the-future-church-in-america/.

About the Author

Dr. Dorothy Oden is a life-long learner. She has been a proponent for education in the underserved and under privileged communities in North Philadelphia. She has taught literacy programs and General Education Diploma (GED) classes for the city of Philadelphia Mayor's Council on Literacy to enrich lives, improve academic scores, and broaden the horizons of teenagers and adults.

She has spent decades working untiringly in numerous positions in her church, evangelizing in street ministry, cooking food for homeless shelters, and supporting faith based organizations.

Dr. Oden holds the following degrees: bachelor of science in nursing, master of education in administration, master of science in adult continuing education, and a doctorate in theology, a PhD.

She is married to Bishop Gerald Oden, pastor of Mt. Zion Apostolic Church of Christ, and they have three married adult daughters and three grandchildren.

www.ingramcontent.com/pod-product-compliance
Lightning Source LLC
Chambersburg PA
CBHW020557160726
47991CB00002B/756

9798891301009